Lalin Bonheur
Bewitched by Talons

Lalin Bonheur
Bewitched by Talons

Margaret O. Howard

APALACHEE PRESS
TALLAHASSEE, FLORIDA 2020

Copyright © Margaret O. Howard 2021
All rights reserved under
International and Pan-American Copyright Conventions.

No portion of this book may be reproduced in any form without the written permission of the publisher, except by a reviewer, who may quote brief passages in connection with a review for a magazine or newspaper.

Cover Photo: "New Orleans Door" by Margaret H. Trammell
Author photograph: Katie Clark
Cover and text design: Carol Lynne Knight
Type Styles: titles set in YanaR and text set Minion Pro;
    cat ornament by Carol Lynne Knight

Library of Congress Cataloging-in-Publication Data
Lalin Bonheur: Bewitched By Talons by Margaret O. Howard – First Edition

ISBN – 978-0-940821-17-0

Apalachee Press Inc. is a nonprofit corporation.
Web site: www.apalacheereview.org

Published in the United States
by Apalachee Press
Tallahassee, Florida
First Edition, 2021

*For my parents
who gave me so many
wonderful opportunities*

*I THANK MY SON, MICHAEL TRAMMELL,
FOR HIS EXPERT EDITORIAL
ASSISTANCE AND EXCELLENT INPUT.*

PREFACE

New Orleans has always been my favorite city. It breathes the mystery and romance that began in my first novel, *Lalin Bonheur*. This sequel, *Bewitched by Talons,* offers me another chance to write about my character, Lalin, a beautiful, gifted mixed-race girl, who lived in New Orleans in the early 19th century. I've heard her voice in my head over the last few years. This may make me sound a bit deranged, but it inspired me to write about her.

Her story begins with the magic remedies she learns from her Grandmother Selene. She helps cure many of her followers in the French Quarter and surrounding bayous with her herbs and potions. At the age of eighteen, Lalin becomes the prized mistress of a young Frenchman, Etienne Legendre. As her protector and supporter, he cares for her safety and quality of life.

When the *loup garou,* shapeshifting wolfmen, decide to steal the magical powers Lalin possesses, their romance is threatened. In fact, their very lives are overcome with danger. When the *loup garou* men overwhelm, Etienne, their struggle with Lalin, a mysterious doctor from France, Lycus Volcain, and a parish priest evolves into an incredible adventure.

Lalin's second gift, the ability to shapeshift into feline form as a small, sleek tuxedo cat enables her to travel the French Quarter and other areas to seek and spy on the evil *loup garou* and a young woman who assists them.

The history of 19th century New Orleans intrigues me with its mix of French Creole heritage, voudou magic, free people of color and their racial hierarchy. This story is carried by the rich culture of this enigmatic city, alive with magical realism, almost two hundred years ago.

— Margaret O. Howard, 2020

CHAPTER ONE

I hear a scratching sound at my louvered door. Could be a stray dog, I think, but, when I turn the lock on the inside door and swing it open, a folded paper falls on the threshold. A note from someone. Peeking through the louvers, I don't see anyone on the banquette, the walkway, outside my house, so I unfold the missive.

> *Mon cher Lalin Bonheur,*
> *You don't know me, but I believe you knew my sister, Sanité Carriere. We need to talk, you and me. I have important information for you. It concerns your safety in the city.*
> *I will be at the market at noon with my wares. My stand is at the back behind the rows of fruits and vegetables. I am near the herbs. My sign states "My Potions Bring Health and Happiness to All." Please meet me. I promise you'll not be sorry.*
> *Apolline Carriere*

"Such a strange note," I whisper. Walking back through my house, I read the message one more time. My clock shows me that I have one hour until noon. I haven't time to consult Etienne, my protector, about this meeting. I know I must think what to do. He's warned me many times that I need to consider my decisions. In these days in our city, there's always dangers. He says, "*Many thieves roam the Quarter in New Orleans in the 1840s. Never open the door for someone you don't know. Don't move rashly,*" he says. "*You depend too much on your mystical visions, Lalin. Not everything is ruled by magic.*"

I sit for several minutes on my chaise longue to consider. It's true that I didn't really know the Sanité. Some say that her magic came from evil sources.

Still she had quite a following, and when she burned to death in a raging fire that night a year ago, many good folks mourned her passing.

If what this Apolline Carriere says is true, then it sounds as if she wants to be a friend to me. What harm can come to me at midday with many shoppers at the market? I reach for the amulet I wear around my neck. St. Michael protects me from all dangers. I say a quick prayer to him and go to change my clothes to meet Mme. Carriere at the market.

It's nearly noon when I reach the Rue Levee. Many people of color shop for their mistress of the big house. Some white Creoles mingle in the crowd. Mostly women buy goods here this time of day. Creole ladies lift their long skirts to keep them from skimming over dirt and grim on the market floors. Most of them carry baskets to store their purchases. Carriages wait along the street for the wealthy, so they can easily bring the foods and fabrics they acquire to their homes.

I stroll among the vendors and make my way towards the back to find Mme. Carriere. Here among the stalls the heavy smells of sweat and ripening fruits mingle with humid air. Tables full of color crowd all around me. Already I've passed pretty fabrics. Solid silks and cotton prints with flowers in shades of blue, purple, red and yellow are displayed for Creole ladies to make their dresses. Around me now are fruit sellers with bananas, mangos and even oranges.

"Check my fine fruits and nuts, Mamzelle," one woman calls to me as I pass. Her skin, like dark chocolate, glistens in a shaft of sunlight. I smile at her and stop to look at her display.

"Ah, Madame, I'd like to buy some pecans." I pick out several handfuls from her bin, add them to the cloth bag I carry with me. I pay her with centimes.

Just pass her stand I see signs for herbs and potions, so I try to spot Madame Carriere. One sign says, "My Powders solve all problems." Such claims impress some white Creole ladies. They pick up small bags of gris-gris, hold them to their noses then nod their heads. Many folks believe these mixtures can heal and aid in solving problems.

At last I see her sign. Mme. Carriere surprises me with her looks. She's tall like me, but a bit stout and her skin's a shade darker than mine. I remember her sister, Sanité was a large woman too, but her skin was nearly black. Odd, but it's true that there can be many skin tones even in one family. She wears a long purple skirt and a matching tignon tied tightly around her handsome head.

She seems to recognize me, although I feel certain I have not seen her before. She calls out, "Mamzelle Lalin, I'm thankful that you have come."

I smile at her and extend my hand. "*Enchanté*," I say.

"Ah, you don't remember me, but I came to your last meeting at the Bayou St. John. I didn't introduce myself." She lowers her voice to a whisper, glances over her shoulder at the surrounding vendors and continues. "Some evil omens I've received in recent weeks, and I often fear for safety here in the city."

My heart jumps, as she says these words. I reach for my amulet, hanging on its chain inside my blouse. My fingers tighten around the medal. I ask for St. Michael's guidance. He lets me see a glow around her head. But he also lets me understand that her fear is real. What she says is true, he tells me.

"What's your trouble, Madame? Tell me how I can help." I lean forward and extend my hand again. Small lines spread around her eyes and mouth. Her fingers grasp mine. I feel the trembling in her.

She speaks so low now that I can barely hear her. "They were after my sister, Sanité, before she lost her life in the fire that night." Again, she turns her head to survey the crowd. "They look to take control of all the mystic powers in the city. My magic has its limits. I came from San Domingo only last year, so I know little of my sister's work with her followers. But they believed that I also had a relationship with you and..."

Her whispers come so fast that I can hardly understand her. "Who are *they*? Speak slowly and please explain."

"The loup garou, Lalin. Two of them have approached me. They come to me in their human form. Good-looking fellows, but they have the single eyebrow that extends above their nose. They have the hair on their palms too. Sometimes they shave it off, so there's no chance they can be recognized."

"Yes, yes, I know who they are. But why do they approach you concerning me? I've never met you."

"Not sure, but from what I hear from several of my sister's followers these shape shifters had been in contact with her. At first, she spoke with them, and they convinced her that their intentions were of a kindly nature. Her magic only turned bad when she lost her temper. In general, her charms and potions brought blessings. Later they tried to turn her rituals to their advantage and..."

"Wait," I say, and raise my hand to let her know I must interrupt. "So, then it's true that Sanité's magic took an evil turn?" The rumors of a wicked influence always followed her. I must know the truth about the woman's magic. I pause and wait to hear her sister's response.

Apolline licks her lips and holds me with a long look before continuing. "I can't deny it from what I hear, but I had only just arrived in the city. I studied with her to learn about her spiritual powers but only for a short time. I wasn't there when the fire came and killed her. Such an awful night."

"But what do you know of the evil in her rituals?" I watch her closely now. She locks her fingers and brings her clasped hands to her chin, as if she's about to pray.

"She did meet with the loup garou. They wanted to learn all the details of her powers. But once she realized that they were in cahoots with your *Tante*

Corinne, and the Papa Lamba, she backed away. Of course, those loup garou became angry at rejection and turned against her. After that they planned to do her in."

Memories come to me as I listen to her. Recollections of the times my Aunt Corinne and Papa Lamba conspired against me with the loup garou run through my head. These thoughts bring back the images from all those months ago. It's painful and frightening to recall. Corinne attacked me with Papa Lamba's assistance. I was able to defend myself, and fortunately I survived with few injuries. Those two were discovered by the police, and now they are in jail awaiting trial.

It's time for me to question this woman, Apolline, and find out exactly why she's felt a need to contact me. "Was my name mentioned in the dealings with the loup garou? Please tell me all you know. I understand you feel that these creatures brought the evil to your sister." With my amulet held in my one hand, I pray my saints give me a sign that I can trust this woman.

If she notices I close my eyes for several minutes, she says nothing. My spirits bring me visions, pictures in my head. I see Apolline with her sister. The image shows me how she cringes in the presence of the loup garou. I don't think this woman's lying, but I will proceed slowly until I can be sure.

"When did these shape shifters contact you to find me?" I ask.

"They only know that your magic is the strongest in New Orleans. You've healed many of your followers. And a number have changed their luck with the charms and spells you give."

I smile at these sweet compliments, but I must pursue the negative, to see what I face. "Do these creatures plan to destroy me? Were they involved in the murder of my protector's wife, Minette?"

"I'm not certain of their methods, but I do know this, when they came to me, they made it clear that they aimed to take control of all the mystic powers in the city. Your name was mentioned above all others." She sighs, shakes her head, and knots her fingers into fists. "They offered me money to help them find your greatest weaknesses."

CHAPTER TWO

Before our meeting ended, Apolline told me that she would make a map for me. At home she has pen and ink. With the information from these men she can figure out the directions to some location in the woods along one bayou road. They told her that's the place to meet with them. The description they gave includes a small cabin. Although she admits she's not been there, they mentioned many details of the location.

"It's on a side road near Bayou St. John. There's a small clearing around the hut, but it's hidden from the road by thickets and giant trees. They told me," she says, pressing prayer hands to her lips, "because I agreed to assist in their plans. It's one reason they pursue me now. They know I'm avoiding them. And even though I never tried to find this place, they're threatened, since I have the directions to their hideaway."

* * *

Etienne comes to me late tonight. We exchange some kisses and then I pour us each a glass of wine. I give him time to rest from his day of meeting customers and writing documents for the family shipping business. But after one more glass of wine, he's most relaxed. He leans back against my sofa cushions and stretches his arms wide. I smile because I know what that gesture means. Time for me fall into his embrace.

I hesitate to ask him questions. Instead I cuddle close to him. My hair is loose around my shoulders. He winds strands of it around his fingers. Now he covers me with kisses. We lay entwined together on the couch and soon caresses blossom into passion. We make love right there on my parlor sofa. It's happened many times before.

I planned to tell him of my meeting with Apolline Carriere, but not tonight. To disturb the mood for our romance would surely be a sin, so I lead him to my boudoir for the night.

✶ ✶ ✶

This early morning, while I brew the coffee, I hear his footsteps behind me. His hands massage my shoulders. I feel his beard against my neck.

"You're up at dawn, *mon cher*. I thought you'd need more sleep," I say. His lips brush against my shoulder, and I almost spill the hot cafe that I just poured.

"I missed you in the bed," he says, "when I reached for you, no one was there." He takes the cup from my hand and puts it on the table, gives me one long kiss and then steps back. His fingers lift my hair up around my ears. His gleaming white teeth spread a smile across his face. "Your beauty never ceases to amaze me."

I laugh, "Flatterer! You know your handsome face made me fall in love with you that night when I came out at the Quadroon Ball. You could have any girl in this city."

"Ah, there's no one but you for me." Now he laughs too. "With all this sweet talk we begin our day."

We sit for a while at my small breakfast table. He tells me plans that he has for the day. His papa's office will be busy sorting through some imports. A large shipment arrived at the docks. The cotton must be readied for its export overseas.

While he talks, I listen, but thoughts of our first meeting flow through my head. That very night he chose me and became my protector. There could never be a marriage for him and me, but with *plaçage* he takes care of me. I have my house, fine clothes, and all I need.

After two years, Etienne's family insisted that he marry another woman, a Creole girl from their social group. Poor Minette, his wife, was murdered. Although the crime was solved, we still suffer from all the mayhem that followed her sad death. I know he's mine. But he can never marry me. Our love binds us even though the laws stand against us.

When he stops his talking to sip his coffee, I decide to take the time to bring up the subject of Madame Carriere. He listens, raising eyebrows here and there, as I tell him about her note, our meeting, and the story of the map.

"Let me see this message," he says.

I pull the paper from my skirt pocket and hand it to him. "She's very fearful for herself but emphasizes that I may be in danger too."

"These monsters are on the prowl again." He studies the note for several minutes.

"She says that they have only revealed themselves to her in human form. But there have been threats. And she believes, as we suspected, that the loup garou had a part in the fire at Queen Sanité's."

"Hmm, can we be sure that they're the same shape shifters we encountered?"

I nod agreement. "From her descriptions of their appearance, I feel sure she's dealing with Abel." I shiver now to think of how he nearly attacked us at our hideaway on Isle Deniere last winter. If it had not been for our holy amulets and the candle flames, we raised against him, he could have killed us on that very spot.

"How can we be sure that this Apolline is not an accomplice?"

"My vision gave me confidence that she's truthful."

He smiles now and shakes his head. I know what he is thinking. My magic doesn't satisfy him. There're always questions. "Wait before you get too cynical, my love. It's true, you know, that my saints always convince me with their message. Apolline says she'll make a map to give me later with the location of their hideout. She promises to have that ready by tonight."

He leans back in his chair. "So, her claim is that they are out to steal your power. It's supremacy they're after. They plan to take control of all supernatural forces in our city." He sighs, "To think only a few years ago I would've called this a pack of nonsense. But now I realize that your magic can work." He reaches for my hand and squeezes tight enough to cause me pain.

"Well, at least you don't doubt me to the same degree that you once did."

"Still sometimes I have to question these visions of yours," he says. "One thing for certain, Lalin." Pointing to the note she left me, he begins to tap it with his fingers. "If this is to be pursued, you'll not go without me along. I simply won't allow it."

"We'll go together, *mon cher*. We can read the map together as soon as she brings it to me. I only hope we can solve this soon. These loup garou move quickly. I may be followed even now."

"Yes, we must move quickly. I should be able to take the family carriage out tomorrow night."

After Etienne leaves for his office, I dress and decide that I want to pay a visit to my new acquaintance, Apolline. She gave me an address on Rue Dumaine where she has a room.

It's still early in the day. The sunlight has barely reached the tops of buildings to shine down on the banquette. A fine carriage rolls by me, as I set out on foot and turn the corner onto Rue Toulouse. The driver tips his hat, and I realize the man is Armand, a follower of mine.

"*Bonjour,*" I call out to him. This carriage is his own, and I guess he's likely to be picking up some Creoles who arrive by ship along the river.

A cool breeze lifts a strand of hair that's escaped from the tignon wrapped around my head. Quadroons and octoroons like me must cover their hair when walking on the street. I tuck the strand back, pull my shawl tighter on my shoulders to shut out the chill.

One man shovels up manure from the road. Many carriage mules and horses travel through the Quarter. At the next corner, those bad smells are gone. A vendor sells the sweet rice cakes, calas, rusks and bouquets of flowers. The fragrance swirls around me as I pass.

When I reach Dumaine, I check the address I have written on a paper. The house, a small one like mine, with eaves hanging just above the doorway, looks dark from the outside. I knock. A few minutes later the door creaks and slowly opens, but only a crack.

A woman's raspy voice asks, "Who's there?"

"Lalin Bonheur, Madame. Apolline Carriere gave me your address. She said she rents rooms here."

The door swings halfway open. An ancient woman in a housecoat squints at me. Her light brown skin is creased with lines. "Ah, Madame Carriere mentioned that you might be stopping by." The woman leans out the door for a moment, looking along the banquette, then she continues, speaking in a low voice. "She moved last night, Mamzelle. She said she had some trouble in the city and had to find another place to stay. I'm not sure where she went."

"Did she leave a note?" I ask.

"No, she stuffed her carpet bags and left in quite a hurry." The woman nods at me and shuts the door without another word.

So, I think to myself, will this be such a short acquaintance with this Apolline? Still I believe she's honest, and I hope that she will contact me again with the map she promised. While I stand a few more minutes on the walkway, it occurs to me that she may've been approached by those evil ones again a good reason for her to move to another address.

For now, I must go home and begin to prepare for a meeting with my faithful followers this night.

CHAPTER THREE

I hire a carriage for the ride to our meeting place on Bayou St. John. The night is clear and cool. It's near November now, and here in our New Orleans we get a touch of winter this time of year. A silver-slivered moon smiles in one corner of the blackened sky. Stars grow brighter as the darkness deepens. The carriage bumps along the bayou road. This wide trail's covered with dried mud and filled with ruts from many wagon rides along the way.

In the distance lights begin to flicker, as we approach my destination. Small bonfires blaze along the road, so all can find this place. More light glimmers through the trees, and I know that this is the great fire that my people make. It flares in the center of this wide clearing. Voices travel on the breeze.

Many followers come to me tonight. Some arrive on the bayou by skiff, a few groups pull-up in wagons, and others tie their horses to skinny oaks and cypresses near the clearing. Most ask for my help with healing or solving problems in their lives. A few white Creoles come to join me. Still most of my followers are people of color.

Two strong men, Armand, and Charles, lend me a hand as I step from the open carriage. I pay the driver and ask him to please wait. My men escort me through the crowd. Most faces I recognize. Quadroon men and women, dressed well in the fashions of the day, mingle with black Africans and mulattoes. The French Creoles hover in the rear. Some are dressed in white.

"Mamzelle Lalin," they call to me as I pass among them.

"*Danse Calinda,*" one woman, in a long blue skirt, calls out in a strong voice. She sways, waving her arms above her head. Two men join her in the steps and turns. *Danse Calinda* begins with voices singing all around.

My candles glimmer in a circle near the flaming bonfire. The scents of melting wax and smoke float around us. Drummers sit astride their instruments. The pounding resonates through the clearing, rebounding off the wall of trees. More followers step closer and join in the dance with me. We move to the rhythms and the rituals begin.

As I spin and bend my body, the saints ride me. They come to me and give me power. Then I know my work can start. Erzulie gives me strength and healing gifts. It's only through her intercession that I provide for the needs of my people.

The first of many steps into my candle circle. "My child has the fever, Mamzelle Lalin. Please to lend me potions to take this sickness from my baby."

From her description I believe the child may have malaria. Two remedies I give her. Sweet wormwood to steep in water, and for good measure, cinnamon to be boiled and mixed with honey. Both potions the child must drink. With the medicines I supply the problem will be cured.

The bonfire blazes while I continue with my work. The air smells of smoke, but it's a pleasant scent. A few fireflies twinkle in the groves of trees. Dispensing herbs and charms takes two hours. For my work I earn coins and promises of trades from my followers. I thank the spirits for allowing me the knowledge to help these people. Many prayers we make on this night.

But as the line of folks comes to its end, I see one more familiar face. Apolline Carriere steps forward and falls to her knees in front of me. I admit I'm not so surprised to see her here. The thought came to me that she might appear at my bayou meeting. My heart feels relief that she looks well when she looks up at me.

She whispers, "I come to you tonight. We must talk, Mamzelle Lalin."

I bless her with a handful of herbs and speak softly. "Yes, I went this morning to the address on Rue Dumaine. I was told you moved in the night."

"There's too much danger for me in the city. I take a cottage on the back roads, but not for long." She looks around and then points toward the crowd. "Even here my enemies may be watching. Can we talk in private?"

I nod and gesture for her to rise from her knees. Then I turn to my people and tell them that we meet again at this same time and place in two more weeks. "My friends, I thank you once again for coming out tonight." I raise my hands above my head and bow to them.

"*Merci*, Mamzelle Lalin," they call back to me and the crowd disperses.

I watch as some walk across the rough ground to climb into their boats. Others untie their horses to begin the journey home.

At last I turn back to Apolline Carriere. My carriage waits nearby, so I invite her to join me there while she tells her story. But she fears that the driver may be listening, so we sit in the forest clearing on stools Armand has brought.

A chill sinks into my skin even though the air is dry. We sit near the bonfire which has been kindled by Armand. For some minutes we rest in silence. I adjust my shawl around my shoulders and wait for her to speak.

"I have made a map," she says. "It shows the whereabouts of the shapeshifters, the loup garou. As I told you, they had for some years been after my sister, Sanité, to include them in her rituals. At some point she gave in, but only for a short time. Once she understood their true aims, she banned them from her meetings. By that time, they had already approached the Papa Lamba and your Tante Corinne. They plotted to steal my sister's magic and her followers." She pauses when we hear twigs crackling behind us.

It's my assistant, Armand, who lingers to make sure we're safe. He waits at a distance, so she continues. "See on this paper." She unfolds her hand-drawn map. "They stay most times at this cabin in the woods just some few miles from here. There's been rumors that a white Creole woman sometimes visits them there, but that I don't know for sure."

I still wonder how it is that she knows so much about these two. Some information she's keeping to herself. Even though my saints have given me the sign that she tells the truth, it's time for me to ask more questions.

"So how is it that you know such details about these creatures?"

Her lips tighten into a frown. "You must trust me, Lalin. These men are sly. They charmed me into thinking that they were my friends even though I thought they were the ones who turned against my sister. They have their ways to attract you."

"They did attract you then. I thought something was missing from your story."

She looks down at her knees, shakes her head, and when she looks up at me again, I see her eyes are wet. She wipes a tear from the side of her nose.

"You guess right, Mamzelle. And I'm ashamed to confess I did. The most handsome called Abel romanced me. They both have charm and captivating ways. I had little money, and he helped me find a place to stay. I swear he hexed me. Made me believe that Sanité had been mistaken about his intents."

"Ah, did you begin an affair with him? Did it go that far?" I ask.

"A brief romance. It lasted for only a few days and then I broke away from him." She bites her lower lip and falls silent.

"What happened? I need to hear the whole story."

Apolline clears her throat, turns her head to make sure Armand has kept his distance. "One of my sister's followers came to me. She expressed much fear for me. Her guess was that they planned to make me one of them. At first, I couldn't believe her. My attraction blinded me to his evil." She hesitates, presses both hands against her forehead and draws a deep breath.

I sit in silence for some few minutes before I speak, "You must have been sick with fear, but her story did convince you. What happened after that?"

"He didn't visit me that night, but I had a strange dream. It was a nightmare really. In the dream, he came to me with all his sweet talk. He began to kiss me. I was pleasured by his lips against my neck." She stops, looks at me with wide eyes then reaches for my hand. "I swear I felt his teeth dig in my skin. When I tried to struggle free, it was too late. My blood flowed from the puncture wounds." Now she releases my hand and rubs her neck.

I lean forward to see if there are signs of breaks in her skin. If she was bitten, she could have the curse they carry. But her neck looks smooth. "You're sure it was a dream then?" I ask.

"*Mon Dieu*, I'm thankful the woman came to me. After that, his spell on me was broken. I moved from those rooms the next day and into the house on Rue Dumaine."

"And the threats began?" I ask.

"Yes, they saw me at the market. I tried to hide from them, but they followed me, and I was cornered. Fortunately, I made sure that several other vendors saw me, so they acted friendly. Still they made their threats in whispered voices."

I watch her movements. She closes her eyes for a moment and presses three fingers to her lips. It's then I ask, "They threatened you with harm. What exactly did they say?"

"They said, if I would cooperate with them, they wouldn't harm me. It was you they wanted. *You must befriend her,* they said. Out of fear I agreed to make a contact with you, but I think by now they know that I betrayed them. I must stay hidden or they'll surely try to punish me."

"You must wear a cross at all times. It will help to keep you safe," I tell her.

She reaches for my hand again. "Do you have one for me?" she asks. "I have no money to buy one."

I smile at her and squeeze her hand. "I think I may have a silver one at home. If you want it, tell me where I can meet you."

"I must stay in hiding for a few days, but, yes, I would be pleased to have it, if you aren't afraid to meet me."

"No, I can't live in fear of loup garou. We'll meet in a few days when you feel safe to leave your hideout." I remind her of my address on Rue Burgundy.

"Mamzelle Lalin, I'm grateful that you accept me. Can I repay you with some assistance?"

"Perhaps we can work together to stop this evil that haunts us both. But for now, I'll say goodnight."

I wish her a safe night, and we go our separate ways. She has her skiff, a boat to travel in, and a lantern to light her way. Soon she's out of sight, disappearing in the darkness. The bonfire I leave for Armand. He'll put it out, after he escorts me to my carriage. We walk together and wish each other a good evening.

I ride now to the center of the city, where my protector, Etienne Legendre, waits for me at home.

CHAPTER FOUR

It's late when I reach my house on Rue Burgundy. I think for certain that my love will be sleeping. But instead he stands near the door.

"I've been worried, Lalin." He frowns, sips red wine from a crystal glass, and then puts it on a nearby table.

I lower my head, as if to bow to him. "*Mon cher*, I hate to think I worry you. Remember with my magic and my amulet I'm most secure, even when I travel on my own."

He grabs me then with such forceful arms that I almost topple over. He staggers a bit himself to keep me from falling. We both begin to laugh, as we stroll through my small foyer into the parlor.

"It's been a busy night," I say, as I pour myself a glass of wine. "I had one surprise. Madame Carriere appeared at my meeting." I pull the map out of the pocket of my skirt and hand it to him.

We sit down together on my parlor sofa. Snuggling against his shoulder, I watch while he studies the map. His eyes widen, and he nods slowly.

He taps one finger against his lips before he speaks, "Hmm, it lacks some details, but I guess it could be used to find the place. You're thinking we need to plan a visit to this hut to spy on these fellows."

"If they're so anxious to gain the secrets of my power, I think we have to learn all we can about them."

"I agree," he says, "but there's a chance they may not even be there when we go. Will your saints show you that the men are at this place, so we won't have a wasted trip?"

An almost smile curls his lips. He taunts me I suspect, but I have a ready answer. "I can pray to the Blessed Mother to give a vision of the location. But even if there's no one at the cottage, it's an opportunity to explore the place. I've seen the fear they give Apolline Carriere, and it's likely that they had some part in her sister's death. They plan to steal the secrets of the magic." I must convince my Etienne that the loup garou want control of me. There's no doubt that our lives may be threatened by these creatures. He worries for me, but I know he's always cynical about my talents.

With raised eyebrows, he blows some air between his teeth. "I know, I know. But sometimes it's still hard to realize that these monsters exist even though I've seen their claws and fangs in action."

No doubt memories of the night they chased us in our feline form on Rue Rampart are stirring in his mind. By climbing over a courtyard gate, we managed to get away from them, but still they did claw my paws before we reached the top. What an evening that was! The same night we had been to a ritual meeting. We barely escaped from a fire that erupted at Queen Sanité's gathering. It was in fact the night she burned to death.

"Ah, so it comes back to you, Etienne. The claws and snarls, my wounded foot. We escaped without serious injuries at least."

He nods, "It's true." He takes my hand and kisses it. "One or both of us could've been mangled, even killed, that night."

"You'll get your family carriage for us to travel in. What night can we make the trip?"

"Tomorrow. I think the sooner we move to learn what's going on with our friend, Abel, the better off we'll be."

* * *

Etienne arrives on time, but I'm already halfway out the door before he enters. It's damp and cool. I wear my woolen cape. My dark hair falls loose around my shoulders, but I cover my head with a shawl to cut out the coldness. A misty rain falls on us as we make our way to his open carriage. The sky's black except for some reflections on the clouds from the lanterns burning at corners where the roads meet.

My love boosts me up into the carriage seat then climbs in on the other side. He lifts the reins and, with this signal to his horses, we are off down Rue Burgundy. After a sharp turn at the corner, the ponies trot on through the Quarter and towards the outskirts of the city.

Almost an hour later we stop along a narrow roadway, which winds through lines of giant oaks. I hold the map up to our lantern. We have made several wrong turns in the darkness, but this time we agree that we're near our destination.

"Look here," I say, pointing to the small square drawn on the paper. "This spot shows the cabin. If we tie up the horses now, we should find a trail leading to their cottage somewhere within this oak grove. We need to go on foot from here on."

He takes the map and stares at the markings for a moment, then raises the lantern up above his head to cast light around the area. We can barely see the outline of the vacant hut in this darkness.

"Yes, it looks right," he says.

"There's one thing we need to agree on now." I reach into my pocket for one bag of gris gris. This one carries mystical powders that we need to complete our goals tonight. "Once we find the trail, we have to take our feline shapes. In our disguise, even if we're seen, we can't be recognized."

His eyes go wide, and he hesitates. He wants to object to shifting. But instead he just groans, "I should have known that was coming. You're right. It will be safer for us to sneak round unseen with those small furry bodies."

"Let's make sure you have your gold cross to wear even in your cat form. We need it for protection."

Etienne climbs down from the carriage and leads the horses off the narrow road. He reaches up to help me down and says, "I tie the horses here, but we must wait to make our change. That strange trick would surely spook the animals. If they get agitated by an orange tabby, they'll break loose and gallop off into the woods."

He makes me laugh when he says that. "I see your point. We'll change ourselves after we're on the trail."

Soon we're off to find the mystery route to the cabin in the clearing. This trail's covered with vines and fallen branches. It'll be easier for us to travel through all this with smaller shapes. As cats, we can crawl under branches rather than tripping over them.

"Are you ready?" I ask, since we have come some distance and are out of sight of the horses with the carriage.

"I think I have no choice," he shrugs.

"You'll be first, so I can make sure you've come through alright. I'll take your gold cross now, so that I can place it around your furry neck." I say my prayers, while I sprinkle him with the powder. Within a few minutes, he begins his transformation. I watch his body shrink, his arms and legs grow shorter and orange fur sprouts through his skin. His nose goes pink. White whiskers poke around his nose. It happens quickly. My ginger tabby is complete. He rubs his back against my leg. Time for me to put the cross around his neck again. I double up the chain, looping it over the peaks of his ears.

With one deep breath I pray again to Erzulie and St. Michael. "Let me join him with my transformation. And thank you for all your blessings. Please keep us safe, my holy saints."

My heart takes somersaults inside my chest. My body's melts from the inside outwards, and as it does, I fall to the ground. My coat, a glossy black and white, comes through my skin. It takes only minutes for my feline-self to form completely. I shake myself and swish my tail.

With legs and paws intact, we stretch our bodies. We test our new feline voices, and, yes, we're ready to communicate. I've managed to keep my amulet around my neck through this whole process, so we're ready to begin our adventure.

Off we go, scampering under broken limbs and a maze of leafy vines. There's still a misty rain to keep us damp. As we proceed, a heavy fog creeps off the nearby bayou. Luckily, we have our good night vision to keep us to our route. In our human form we'd be nearly blinded by the fog.

My ginger tabby leads the way, but I scurry right behind him. He hits a sudden skid in front of me, sliding to a stop. Some bright yellow eyes glare at us from just ahead along the trail. We freeze. Etienne turns around to warn me of this possible danger. Whatever's on the path has frozen on its spot.

I tap Etienne on the back with my paw, whispering in our private language, "Could be a raccoon or fox."

His whiskers twitch, but then he moves bravely forward. I follow and we hear a scrambling sound ahead. The animal jumps aside. There's a rustling through the vines and brambles, so we proceed again. It's a least a mile or two before we see what looks like a clearing in the trees. A flash of night sky looms out ahead of us. One quarter moon spreads light behind a thinning patch of clouds. Yes, we have reached the clearing on the map.

The open space is wider than I expected, and sure enough the small cabin sits at the far end. Behind it more oaks and cypress trees reach upwards to the night sky. I suspect the bayou lurks only a short distance from that forest wall.

We pause now to make decisions on what our next move should be. After a short discussion in our feline language we conclude that we must get as close to the hut as possible. There's a window on one side, and we can see light shining through the glass panes. If lanterns burn inside, it's highly probable that someone's home.

Slinking along the edge of the forest undergrowth, we pad our way toward the dwelling. As we draw closer, we can see a wooden barrel near the window. If one or both of us can leap to the top, we can do the spying that we came for.

When we reach the barrel, Etienne sits back on his haunches to make ready for his jump. I watch him dig his claws into the top edge and climb up. He crouches low, but I know he's peering in the window now. I wait for him to turn back towards me, but he keeps his facing to the window. I must join him. By his pose I know that they're inside the cottage and he's watching them.

Up I spring with my front paws extended, claws ready to pull me up. My tabby barely moves his eyes toward me even now. I squeeze beside him to get a view of what goes on inside. To my surprise there are three people in this one room. Abel and his male companion sit at a wooden table. I can't see Abel's face because his back is to the window. His friend looks as though he could be a brother. He's a young man like Abel with dark brown hair, attractive features and even at this distance I see his forehead with the eyebrows meeting just above his nose. A loup garou for certain.

The big surprise is that a woman stands between their chairs. She shakes a finger at Abel. He nods his head, but even though our feline sense of hearing is acute, I hear nothing but the raindrops falling on the barrel.

The woman's dressed in fashions of the day. Her dark hair, swept up in a twist, shines in the lantern glow. She appears to be a white Creole like the men. Ah, for one instance now, she turns in profile. It's such a quick view that I can't describe her clearly and yet there's something familiar. Etienne seems entranced. I wonder if he hears something that escapes me. I tap him softly with one paw. He spins his head around, but only for a second. His tail slaps against the barrel, and I know that he's detected something.

While we crouch there on the barrel, the wind picks up, racing through the branches of the trees above. A stroke of bad luck happens just then. One long dead branch breaks off the top of a giant oak. We both look up when we hear the crack. The limb circles in a swirling breeze for a moment then spirals downward toward the barrel we're perched on. In an instant my ginger tabby and I fly off our viewing spot onto the ground. I take off, thinking he's right behind me. It's certain that the loup garou will hear a crash outside their window.

I spot a fallen tree trunk just ahead. At one end there's an opening where it's rotted out. With all the speed I can manage, I squirm inside the space that's barely wide enough for me. Rounding my small body into a tight squeeze, I wait for Etienne to join me. With my ears perked up, I listen. Hearing nothing, I peek out the hole. No ginger tabby. Where is he?

Just then I see a flash of light from the corner of my eye. Thinking there may be lightning from the sky, I draw back, but there's no thunder. I crane my neck to see out again. What I see makes my furry tail bush out.

Abel stands at a distance from the cabin window. A lantern he placed on the ground. But it's what he has in his arms that makes my heart tumble. No, no, no, this can't be! I hiss and dig my claws into the tree trunk where I'm hiding. The man holds a bundle that looks like orange fur. Nearby the dead branch lies broken on the ground. My guess is that the limb or parts of it hit my tabby. I don't see him struggling in this wolf man's arms. He's limp, but strong instincts let me know he's alive. He must be stunned or injured.

Abel marches to the cabin door with my tabby clutched in his arms. In he goes and the door slams closed.

CHAPTER FIVE

Thunder roars so loud the ground shakes around me. I shiver, crouching in the downpour that follows. Limbs come crashing down on all sides. Taking shelter once again, inside the dead tree trunk, I wait out the storm. It takes perhaps an hour before it passes. Finally, I can creep out from my hiding place.

I see the oil lamps still burn inside the cabin. My fears make me feel sick, but I know I must keep going. I slink through the trees.

The sky grows brighter as the rainclouds separate and drift beside the moon. A few stars sparkle against this night sky. I must get back to the cabin window. The barrel remains standing with broken branches scattered all around it. I make my way through the brush. Something glimmers in the darkness. As I creep nearer, I see the gold cross. It must have fallen from my love's neck when we scrambled off the barrel. Clearly, he's without this divine protection. I manage to unhook the chain with my claws. With a flip of one paw I let it fall around my neck, breathe a small relief, and move on.

When I reach the window, I leap up once again to see what's happened to my Etienne. I clench my tiny teeth and pray, "Please, please, St. Michael protect him from these creatures."

The two men and the woman sit together at the table, their backs to me. They're talking, but I can't hear their words. I scan the room. Where is he? Let me see a flash of orange fur. Several minutes pass. I tremble, fearing for his life.

Ah, I spot him. He lies still beneath the table, then I see his tail wag. A saucer lies to one side. So, he appears unharmed. I suspect they plan to make a meal of him at some point. But, thank *mon Dieu*, their intuition hasn't given them a clue to his identity. No doubt he won't last long if they discover his human form.

My body aches with exhaustion from all the tensions of this night. At last I curl up to keep watch for the night. Although I strain to stay awake, I lose myself and drift into sleep.

At dawn I wake to the creaking of the cabin door. Startled by the sound, I jump and tumble off the barrel. Landing on my paws, I dart into the nearby grove that's thick with cypress trees. Back arched and peeking from behind an oak, I see Abel standing by the door. But what I also see, makes me purr. My ginger tabby saunters out, swishing slowly through the grasses near the stoop. Abel disappears, and he's left the door open just a crack. Perhaps they think this cat they found needs to relieve himself. But there's no time for me to guess what they might be doing next.

I dash from my hiding place and call to my Etienne in our private language. Thank Erzulie, he sees me and in an instant, flies across the clearing until he reaches me. I lick his ears and brush my nose against his whiskers. He signals me that he has only a few scrapes along his back. His injuries are few. I use my tongue to brush away the pains he may be having from his scratches.

"It's time for us to leave," he purrs. "As long as they think they had a visit from a stray tabby, we've no worries."

Without looking back, we scurry off with all the speed we can muster. Bounding over logs and tangled brush, we sometimes skid on wet leaves along the forest floor. At last we reach the dirt road. My ginger tabby looks both ways. He gets his bearings and scampers over ruts and puddles with me at his tail. Finally, we see our carriage still parked where we left it, but the horses have broken loose.

"We change shape quickly," he says to me. "My horses come to me, if I can find them in the woods."

"My saints, please bless me with the change I need." The shift comes quick, and I use my magic to give Etienne his human form with some speed.

We stand together now and have a long embrace before he takes off through the trees to find our ponies. I hear him whistling. The sound of hooves echoes down the road. We're in luck. I need to get away as soon as possible. Even though the loup garou didn't discover us, they may go looking for the orange tabby outside the cabin. The evening comes as I wait and listen. When I think of all the fears of the past night, I realize that it's more luck than magic that's kept us safe. But still without our ability to shift our shape, we could never witness all we saw. This day passed like the wind rushing through the trees.

The whistling stops and the neighing of the horses grows closer. He's leading them back to me and our carriage. I whisper thanks to all my saints. They blessed us with their protection once again.

Etienne comes through the trees, leading his team with a link of rope. "I'll repair these harnesses with some strips of leather, and we'll be off," he says.

While he fits the harness on one horse, I hold the other by a leather strap. He hitches both to the carriage and helps me climb up to the passenger side. In the distance sounds catch my ears. Voices echo through the woods.

"Do you hear that?" I whisper to Etienne. "Could it be them?" I clutch his hand.

He lifts the reins, clicks his tongue, and the horses trot forward. Sloshing through the puddles, we go at top speed. "Who knows? I wonder if they would be so concerned about a fluffy tom-cat." He shrugs, but his smile lets me know his feeling of relief.

I keep watch on the way. No lights are flashing through the forest, but still some sounds rebound off the trees. Was that a howl I heard? I stare off into the darkness. My neck grows tight with tension, as we swerve around a limb lying on the road. Please, Erzulie and St. Michael, protect us from all evil. I reach for my amulet and lift it to my lips. My saints relieve my fear, but still we have some miles to go before we reach the city.

Something moves in the brush just to one side of us. In my haste to signal Etienne, I cry out too loudly. Startled now, he jerks the reins. Our horses rear up and almost throw us off the carriage seat. Two fawns run out between the trees. Etienne holds the ponies back, while these young creatures bound across the road in soaring leaps. Their spindly legs stretched out almost straight as they fly through the night landing somewhere in the brush.

What a deep breath I take now. My love turns to me and smiles. I laugh out loud, clapping my hands together with relief. "Amazing, that two baby deer gave me such a panic."

✳ ✳ ✳

An hour later we reach the Legendre home on Rue Esplanade. Nearly all the houses are dark this time of night. One oil lamp burns in a window here and there. Etienne takes the carriage up the drive and stables the horses for the night. He thinks it's good for us to take a stroll to my house instead of dropping me off at my front door.

"It's a precaution," he says. "I didn't want to leave you alone tonight, even for the short time it takes me to bring the carriage back to my family's home." When he says this, he drapes one arm around my shoulders, leans forward and gives me the sweetest kiss I can imagine.

"All my love for you and, as always, I thank you." I return his kiss and we embrace before we venture out onto the banquette.

Holding hands, we hurry across Esplanade and on to my house on Burgundy. It's not so many blocks. Happily, the moon breaks through the clouds to give us light. The streets are quiet tonight and we reach my door without a problem.

Once inside we lock up for the night. I check his back to see the cuts he has from the large tree branch that fell on him. While cleaning these small wounds with my homemade herbal balm, I ask him to tell me what he found out inside the hut last night.

"Perhaps tomorrow's a better time to discuss those details," he says, while I dab balm lightly on his cuts.

"I guess you must've learned something about the strange woman with them in the cabin. I thought she might be Abel's sister."

He surprises me with the look he gives me now. His frown lets me know that I've made some mistake. "You didn't see her. I thought you knew." His gruff tone is unexpected.

"No, Etienne, I never saw her face. I don't understand. What's wrong?"

CHAPTER SIX

He glares at me; his lips twisted in an odd way. Then he whispers, "Lalin, the woman's not a stranger."

"What?" I ask.

"She's Madame's niece." He shakes his head, as if it's me who's annoyed him.

"*Mon Dieu*, Etienne, are you certain? The plump Yvette, who bewitched you last year in Natchez?" Right then the moment in the bayou woods comes back to me. Yes, I do recall thinking that she looked familiar, when she turned her profile to the window."

Bad memories fill my mind. Last year, that white Creole woman, Yvette, tried to steal my Etienne from me. It was a time when we left New Orleans after all the sadness and stresses of my protector's wife's death. We decided to take a steamboat up the river.

At the small town of Bayou Sara, we left the ship to start a new life on a plantation. Etienne gained employment, and we stayed for some months. During that time, my saints brought me dreams of Grandmam Selene lying sick in her bed. Of course, I knew that I must leave to care for Grandmam in New Orleans.

It was then that the plump Yvette came to visit her aunt, Madame Nanette, the owner of the plantation, Bon Aimée. My Etienne worked as manager for the widowed lady, so he remained there to keep his job. In my absence Yvette took a fancy to my handsome protector and used some wicked magic to put a spell on him.

These depressing memories bring me tension. My muscles tighten as I strive to maintain composure and realize this scheming woman is here in New Orleans. Trouble has followed us to the city.

I'm not surprised, when Etienne shifts his eyes to the floor. He takes a deep breath, and mutters, "Indeed, it's her. The news could not get stranger."

And, so it happened, that we stay up until the early hours of the morning. Instead of love talk, we spend our time discussing. I surmise she's here to track him down. What other reason could there be? How is she connected to Abel and his companion? Are they related?

Etienne rubs his palms together, making swishing sounds. I think we need to calm our nerves, so I leave him sitting there and go to pour some wine for us. Soon it will be daylight; we have to face the day without sleep.

"You must have listened to their conversation in that cabin. What were they saying? Was your name mentioned? How is Yvette connected to these men?" I ask.

"No, they gave no clues to their connection. In truth they were talking about your friend, Apolline. Abel and the other man, called Francois, did most of the talking. They've been searching for her new location. Abel said that he felt certain that her powers were limited, but still they couldn't let her get away."

"They didn't mention you or me? Is that correct?"

"Yes, that's right. In fact, they spent some time studying a city map, and then they played cards for half an hour before retiring for the night.

"And she said nothing?" I ask him. "I know she's come to find you. They may plan to kidnap you and make you one of them."

"There are other possibilities," Etienne says. "She could have come to the city for shopping or even on some family business." He pauses, bites his lower lip, and continues, "Madame owns a house in the city that we know."

"Don't talk foolish, Etienne. You know she's here to look for you. You said yourself 'the news could not get much stranger.' And is she like the loup garou? Another shifter? We have to do more spying to get answers and find out what she's planning."

"And we will make those efforts soon, Lalin." He strokes my arm and tries to smile. "I must get a few hours of sleep. I have commitments at the office in the afternoon."

At this late hour, we undress and crawl into my bed, too tired for anything but snuggling close together before falling off to sleep.

* * *

When I wake, Etienne has already dressed in the clean clothes that he keeps in my wardrobe. He tells me to stay in bed and not to worry about giving him coffee and rolls with butter.

"I'll eat later at one of the coffee shops on Rue Royal," he says.

I sit up in bed. "Be most careful, love. Now that we know that woman's here, we must keep a constant watch."

To my surprise he smiles. "She's the least of my worries. It's you that has me most concerned. Stay out of trouble, please." He comes to my bed and bends forward to give me his loving kiss. "See you tonight," he says and then leaves.

Without intention I fall back to sleep, waking in the mid-morning. Soon I'm up to make a pot of coffee and boil the milk. As I am running a comb through my long hair to catch the tangles, I hear a knocking at my front door. It may be one of my followers stopping by to get a remedy or a charm of some sort.

"Who's there?" I call, before I open the inside door.

"It's me, Apolline, come to learn from you."

"Yes, I recognize your voice," I say as I open the door.

She dresses well today with a calico tignon, gold earrings and a brightly printed dress. The fabric shows a mix of yellow colored flowers. Grinning broadly, she asks, "May I come in, Mamzelle Lalin? Or is this a bad time for you?"

I extend my hand to her, and she steps in. "I'm still in my dressing gown as you can see, but I have some coffee ready, if you want to join me in a cup. You can tell more about what you wish to learn."

The coffee and boiling milk I pour into a china pot, and I lead her into my parlor, where I have a tray. "Have a seat, Apolline." I gesture to the sofa, while I settle myself near the table with the tray.

She sits politely. Her hands folded in her lap, while I pour our beverage into my china cups. Then I place one cup into its saucer, passing to my guest.

"Here are some rolls," I say, pointing to a napkin covered basket. "Please help yourself, if you're hungry."

She nods, takes a sip of cafe au lait, and says, "I do, of course, want to learn from you, Mamzelle, but above all else, I hope to assist you in your work in exchange for the instruction."

Truly her words ring a bell for me inside my head. My Tante Corinne once told me something similar, but in the end, I found that she was my enemy. Corinne deceived her own mother, my Grandmam Seline. And she took me close to death. Is this memory connected to my new acquaintance? I wonder if I should doubt her motives.

She continues, "And also important I come to take advantage of your offer. You spoke of a silver cross you could give me to protect myself from the loup garou."

"Ah, yes," I say, "I will get it for you. Any news of those creatures?"

After I get the cross from a table drawer, I show her how to fasten the chain around her neck. I smile at her, and in silence we both sit for several moments. I close my eyes to pray for answers from my saints. *"Can I trust this woman, Erzulie?"* I ask her in my head. Even though I felt assured by my spirits in the past, uncertainty comes back to haunt me. "St. Michael, please give me a sign."

Apolline pulls something from inside a pocket of her dress. At first, I back away, wondering what she's doing. Then I see what she reveals. *Mon Dieu*, a devotional scapular of Our Lady. She lifts it slowly and I see her lips reciting prayers.

She says in a low voice, "The priest gave me this scapular when I confessed to him. He's a kind man and could see how great my fears were. I need all protection I can get."

My Saints choose to answer me with this show of devotion. This woman reveals that her faith, like mine, gives her strength. I make the sign of the cross and bow my head.

She whispers, "I know that you've been tested in your life. You need the kind of reassurance that I also ask for. My sister, Sanité, was led astray before her death. I want answers too. Believe me. My fears are much like yours."

"Yes, it's hard for me to trust these days," I say. "I rely on Etienne and my Grandmam Selene for all advice. But most of all I listen to my Saints when they give answers. As you know, my Aunt Corinne betrayed me. Like you, she once approached with promises of assistance. All she asked for was instruction in my healing gift with the spirits."

"You have reason for your doubts," she nods. "My past connections to the loup garou may give you worries. They did influence me for some brief time, but I now know I must avoid them no matter what they say or do. If you feel you can't trust me, I will understand."

"You've given me your word," I say. "I believe I've had the reassurance I need. Wait here and finish your coffee. I'll change from my night dress then we'll discuss how we might work together.

And so, it is that Apolline comes twice a week to learn how I mix some potions. There are many lessons that I can offer her. In return she brings me herbs that she collects to sell at her stand in the market.

Today makes the third week of our sessions. In this time, we've heard no news of the loup garou. Etienne and I prowl the Quarter in our feline shapes to keep watch for Abel, Francois, and the plump Yvette. There's been no sign of them.

✻ ✻ ✻

Apolline arrives again at my door on schedule. She wears her best clothes for our meeting. My silver cross hangs on its chain around her neck. I find her to be a sweet, kindhearted woman, and my spirits give me renewed confidence in her loyalty.

Today the weather's pleasant, so we take our herbs and mixing bowls out into my courtyard. The sun's already high in the sky, but at a slant this time of year. My one small oak tree casts its shadow across the stones. I have a table set up and we bring two stools to sit on.

"As you know, High John the Conqueror root works for many purposes. I use it in my gris-gris for protection and strength. The Low John root's a little different. It can help with pain in childbirth. I often give it to my followers." While I explain these usages, I take out pieces of the root from my containers. These are wooden boxes that I store my best cures in.

Apolline watches while I take pieces of the root and mix them in an almond oil. I tell her that this mixture must sit in a bottle for at least one week.

"One month would be still better," I tell her.

Just as I say these words, a shadow falls across our table. Oddly, I don't look up right away. The shadow circles on the courtyard stones in a wavy motion. Apolline and I both glance up to see a darkly feathered bird. A blue-gray color glimmers on its feathers. It hovers not far above our heads. Then I see it carries something in its beak. Rising from my stool, I motion to my guest to move back too. The creature drops a large object on the stones near my feet.

"*Mon Dieu*, is that a spider?" I call out in surprise.

CHAPTER SEVEN

Apolline screams so loud it numbs my ears. I stagger back as this hideous creature scurries towards me. It's as big as my hand and has at least eight legs.

"*Bondye,* what is this thing?" I cry.

My companion presses both hands to her lips to stifle one more shriek. I watch her fall backwards as if she may have fainted. Then I come back to my senses and think to grab one of the large bricks that line my garden wall. With all the force that I can muster, I hurl the brick on top of this awful thing.

The monster spider lies still under the brick. Its legs extend out from one side. I run to Apolline, who's sprawled on her back. She bumped her head in the fall, but still is conscious.

"Lie still; lie still," I say and rush into the house to get a cold cloth to wipe the bloody head wound. Inside I wet a small towel and rush back through the French doors. What I see then takes my breath away. This hairy creature has somehow crawled from underneath that heavy brick. It appears to be unharmed and, while I stand in trembling silence, it skitters across the courtyard stones.

I run fast to grab another brick and turn to see the creature's near to Apolline. It's crawling at her right arm. Some blessing from my Saints lets me spy my broom and my sharp-edged hoe propped against the wall. With these two in my hands I fly in her direction. The broom lets me wrangle with the thing. It tries to cling to her brown skin. A second brush catches it from underneath. It spirals in the air for just one moment then lands a few courtyard stones to one side. Dropping the broom, I grasp the hoe with both hands. It clangs against the stones as I hack at its hairy body. Liquids ooze from the nicks and slashes that I make, but there is no more movement.

Immediately I turn to Apolline, who lies groaning on her back. I kneel to wipe her head wound and clean the blood away. It doesn't look too bad. But then I see her jerk her arm. She has the shakes from head to toe.

"The pain, the pain," she cries.

Now I see there are puncture marks on her forearm. These marks turn almost black, and her arm is swelling. "We must get you inside," I whisper.

She's weak but I'm able to help her to her feet. Leaning hard against me, she takes a few steps then nearly topples over. Luckily, I am strong enough to catch her. We both stand still for several minutes.

"Do you think you can get through the doors, if you lean on me?" I ask.

She nods, so we both step cautiously forward. When we reach the portico near my French doors, I pause to let us both take a few deep breaths. At last we're inside and I steer her to my sofa.

I hurry to the cabinets where I keep jars and containers of healing herbs. Vinegar I find, also baking soda, some clean rags, and a small knife. These I carry to the table near my sofa. First the poison stinger must be found and removed. Yes, I see this small thing remaining in the wound. With the sterile knife I pluck out the poison. Then I apply vinegar to cleanse and dab the spot gently with a cloth. Baking soda comes next. This mixture will draw out the poison. If only I had fresh papaya, I would lay a slice of that across the wound, but no papayas grow here this time of year. Instead I decide to make a poultice with a pinch of charcoal dust. Surely all the venom will come out now. Apolline keeps her eyes closed, but her moans show me she is conscious. Her shakes have stopped. She's completely still.

"How is your pain?" I ask.

I wait for her response. She says nothing. I touch her forehead. It feels hot. A fever's setting in. I must think what remedies to use. Ah, an herbal tea with ginger for the fever will help. Also, some valerian root to relax her.

"I'll be right back," I say and lay a cool towel across her arm.

Off I go to my kitchen room. I'm out the door again, but before I reach the kitchen entrance something catches my eye. A small puddle of dark liquid spreads across one courtyard stone, but the creature disappeared. I creep towards the puddle to see more clearly what remains. The fluid looks thick like honey. What I see too are several dark blue feathers stuck around the edges. So, the bird returned to take away the hairy thing. I make a mental note to return and scoop up some of the spider blood or poison to analyze it later.

My first mission is to brew the herbal tea for Apolline to drink. I pray it will suppress her fever and help her sleep.

✱ ✱ ✱

It's past midday now, and Apolline sleeps soundly on my sofa. I hear her heavy breathing. Her forehead still feels hot, but the swelling on her arm has gone down. While I'm placing a fresh cold towel against the wound, I hear a rattle at my street side louvered door. A key turns in the inside door. I turn around to see Etienne walking through the vestibule.

What good luck, I think. He sometimes comes to have a midday meal with me, but today, since we had no plans, I am surprised.

"*Mon cher*, I am blessed that you've come back today this early. Come, come. Apolline's been stung by a huge spider."

"What?" he says and drops his coat and hat on my tea table near the door.

"Like a nightmare the thing appeared. While we mixed our herbs and oils at my table in the courtyard, a giant bird flew down and dropped the monster on the stones. I threw a brick on it, then Apolline fainted and fell backwards on the stones. When I went inside to get some toweling for her head wound..."

"Slow down, slow down, Lalin. You're talking so fast I can barely understand you."

"Shh, I didn't want to wake her," I say pointing to Apolline.

"Yes, I gather that the spider survived the brick and bit your apprentice on the arm." Etienne leans forward looking intently at my friend. "I see some purple streaks on her skin around that towel. How does the wound look?"

"I check every fifteen minutes. My medicine works well. The swelling stopped and, although the skin's still dark around the sting, it looks much better now."

He turns to me and asks, "Do you think it was a black widow spider?"

"All I can tell you is I've never seen an insect that large." I hold my hands apart a space to show him the huge size.

"Hmm," he murmurs, shakes his head, and takes a seat on a nearby chair.

"Don't doubt me. Believe me. It was some supernatural creature. The bird that brought it was the largest I've ever seen. Its feathers like a blue jay, but darker, almost indigo."

"Can I have a look at the remains of this monstrous thing?" he says.

"Ah," I whisper to myself remembering that I wanted to collect the spider's blood off the stones outside. "Stay with Apolline a minute, Etienne. There's some blood or poison on the stones. I must collect to examine later. Nothing left but a spot of blood. The bird flew back while we were inside. It came and took the spider's body." He stares at me in silence, but nods.

I scurry to my shelves to find a small container and a spoon. Out I go through the French doors. Oddly, the pool shrunk to one dark spot. Hardly any liquid's left. I manage to scrap up a few flakes and drop them in the container. Then I notice there are a few dark blue feathers scattered nearby. These I collect and place in the pocket of my skirt.

"Later I'll see Grandmam Selene and have her help me examine these remains. There may be a clue here to what this poison is." I say these words to myself while I go back inside.

"Perhaps we should consult a doctor," Etienne says as I come through the door.

"Believe me. My herbs and poultice will be enough. These medical men are limited in their treatments."

I smile at him now. Even with all the commotion he happened into, he may be hungry. "I have soup on the stove in my kitchen room," I say to him. "Let me ladle out a bowl for you, my love."

He returns my smile, walks towards me for a warm embrace. "You are the perfect woman, my Lalin. Even with this awful story, you still remember that I might be hungry."

I laugh out loud. "And you're my protector, but most of all my lover. I'm always here to serve your needs."

He gives me one long squeeze. Our tensions lift for these few minutes. We share more kisses and he slides his fingers inside my blouse sleeves. "I love your smooth skin," he says.

"Not now, Etienne," I whisper, and, with a sudden twisting turn, I escape from his strong arms. "You must have your soup."

Once again, I check on Apolline to make sure she's sleeping still, before I head for my kitchen room.

* * *

The next hour passes quickly while I serve the crab bisque that I prepared for him. He declares that my cooking is almost as good as my love. We both laugh.

I pour him a cup of chicory coffee, lay out another plate of fruit and cheese and sit next to him while he completes his meal.

" Where am I?" I hear Apolline call from my small parlor.

"I must attend to her," I say and hurry to the room.

She sits up as I enter. Perched on the edge of the sofa, I think for one moment that she may topple over. But no, she sees me, and her eyes go wide. With a straight back she falls against the cushions.

"Something happened," she says. I hear the puzzlement in her voice. "Did I faint? I have no memory of it."

"We had a most unwelcome visitor. Do you remember that?" I ask.

She shakes her head. "You were giving me some instructions in your healing magic. That's the last thing I recall." Her voice sounds weak, but I believe that she's gained back at least a little strength.

"As you say, I started to show how to mix my best herbs, when a large bird came soaring right above my courtyard. It hovered then dived low and dropped an enormous spider on the stones. I tried to kill it with a brick, but in the end the thing managed to bite you on the arm." I pause and give her a chance to answer, but she says nothing. "Then you passed out. I treated you with healing herbs. You've been asleep for quite a while, but it seems your fever's gone for now."

Etienne's joins us in my parlor. "It's good to see you sitting up," he says.

Apolline stares at us in silence for several minutes, and I see the fear reflected in her eyes. Then she murmurs, "I'm afraid I've brought this evil to you, Mamzelle Lalin. I saw this feathered creature once before."

Chapter Eight

The bird that she describes sounds like the one that swooped down on us this forenoon. "It's almost large enough to be an eagle," she says. "Thick indigo feathers. A large beak it had too. It flew into the marketplace last week. First it sailed above my table then dived down and pulled out a strand of my own hair."

"Ah, you know what that means." I shake my head and clasp my hands together. "Someone uses that hair to connect and cast a spell. But who?"

"You can't believe all those old tales," Etienne interrupts my thoughts.

"These things can work, Etienne. It takes some skill to get the best results, but even if a mission fails, there can be damage."

"So, you believe that the bird is one more shapeshifter trying to invade our lives."

"Well, it's clear someone wanted to harm Apolline." I pause and sit down next to my friend. Thoughts tumble in my head. "It's likely that the shifter used the strand of hair to catch the scents of my companion here."

"And now they know where you are too." Apolline bites her lower lip

"You say *they*? Who are you talking about?" I ask.

"I don't know for certain but do suspect the loup garou have some part in this."

Something stirs my memory now. I close my eyes. Erzulie, my blessed saint, has a clue for me. I say a quick prayer and wait for her response. Ah, the recollection takes me back to the bird that brought a scorpion to sting my mother some months ago when we stayed in Natchez. At that time, I had no idea who might be out to harm us. Then I learned that it was my own Tante Corinne who had conspired against me and murdered Etienne's wife to throw the blame on him. I guessed that it must have been her who brought the scorpion that stung Mama. Certainly, that menace was intended for me. I never thought of the woman who bewitched my protector. Could it have been Yvette scheming against us?

"Lalin, what's wrong?" I hear Etienne's voice and open my eyes.

"A memory came to me," I say. "I think I know who's after us. The plump Yvette, she's the one. It's seems clear to me."

"How can you be so sure?" Etienne frowns, showing creases at the corners of his eyes.

"Well, when Mama got stung by the scorpion in Natchez months ago, I had no idea what had happened. But later when we discovered that Corinne was out to do us all harm, we realized that she too was a shifter. She shifts into a bird form. You remember that."

"Now, I see," he says. " You thought that the bird that dropped the scorpion was Corinne."

"That's right, but Corinne's in jail along with Papa Lamba. One more thing, the memory brought me a picture of the bird again. Its thick plumage was a shade of indigo."

"You have me almost convinced," he says. I don't doubt that there's a shifter with all I've seen at this point, but I hadn't thought of Yvette."

Apolline sits still on my sofa. "And she's the woman who's with Abel, the loup garou," she says.

"I have no proof, but, when my Holy Mother, my Erzulie, gives me such a clue, I'm convinced." I lean closer to her. "Apolline are you feeling like yourself again? I think my remedies have done you good."

"Yes, yes," she says, "I should be on my way soon. From the shadows on the courtyard, I see it's long past noon and almost evening."

"But you should stay with me. It's too soon for you to be out of here. In fact, stay until tomorrow morning. I'll make more tea and you can rest."

She smiles at me. "I thank you so much, but I must be going before dark. I will have that tea though before I leave."

The three of us share a pot of tea. I add more herbs to treat her wound and give her a bag of healing powders to take with her.

I hate to let her go out alone after what happened, but Etienne gives us a solution to the problem. He says he will hire a carriage and accompany her to her home.

When they leave, I decide to light candles at my altar. It's time for me to pray. I must consult my spirits before I make my next move.

* * *

My love returns quite late. It seems that Apolline lives quite some ways from the city. I thank him once again for escorting her to her home.

My saints brought me a strange vision while he was gone. Although I like to confide to my love, I hesitate because I'm unsure of the meaning of the images in the dream.

In the vision, the three talk together in the bayou cabin. Abel, Francois, and Yvette are speaking, but I can't hear the words. I pray that the spirits will carry their voices to me. Just then a sound breaks through in the vision. A knock hammers at their door. Abel walks across the room and the door swings open.

The tall, imposing figure of a man strides through the door. His back is turned and his form's dark and shadowy, completely unclear. All I see for sure is that he wears a long winter cape. The three greet him with slight bows. I wonder if he's a relative or benefactor of some sort.

"We're honored by your visit," Abel's voice comes to me.

"Indeed, an honor, Monsieur," Yvette adds a curtsey to her greeting.

I pray this man will turn around, so I may see his face. All four gather around the table in the center of the room.

"We were hoping that you would come to us to support our plans," the other man says.

At just that moment, the impressive man starts to turn his face. But instead of the revelation that I need, I get a strong whiff of smoke. What's burning? I wake on the floor beside my altar. All my candles flare up as if from the wind, but the doors are closed. Worst of all my altar cloth blazes with flames from one candle that's toppled over. I rush to stamp it out and then pour water from a pitcher. The cloth is charred, but at least the danger's gone.

My love observes my trembling, as I recall this near disaster. He must also sense my fears about the vision.

"Lalin, it's been a long day for you. And now you've set a fire with your candles." He comes close to me and checks me for burns.

"I'm fine really. The spirits brought me a disturbing dream. I need some time to consider what it means."

He pulls me close to him and I feel my body melt into the warmth of his strong arms and chest. With one quick scoop, he lifts me off the floor.

"I know some ways to make you forget your worries for at least one night." His kiss fills me with all the blissful pleasure I've felt for him since we first met at the Quadroon Ball three years ago.

Before I can respond to that first kiss, he carries to my boudoir. Everything happens so fast after that I say I lost myself in his embrace and in the happiness that his love brings. He knows every inch of my being. I am consumed, but in the most delightful way.

Chapter Nine

In the morning I describe my vision to Etienne. He sips from his cup and listens. When I finish, he shrugs his shoulders, places the cup in its saucer and reaches across the table to stroke my hand.

"I'm not sure why you're so disturbed by this dream," he says. "It seems to me the worst things that happened yesterday were the giant spider and your altar fire."

"You're right. Those things could have been fatal. I was especially concerned for Apolline." I lean back in my chair. "The reason the vision frightens me is because it brings a threat. Seeing those shapeshifters in their cabin brought a warning that our enemies have plots against us. Remember Apolline first told me; they want to steal my power. And who's this tall stranger that they're bowing to?"

"Hmm," Etienne taps his fingers on the table. "Well, I admit you've been right in some of your suspicions. Perhaps we need to investigate some more. My greatest concern is for your safety, love. These characters are never up to any good."

"Yes, I think we need to take a chance to spy on them again, as soon as you can take time from your work."

"Tomorrow night we'll take the carriage. However, we need to know if they're at the bayou cabin."

I grasp my amulet. "I will take my time today to consult with Grandmam Selene. I have the poison flakes from the spider to show her. Together we'll try to find out what it is." I lift my medal up and point to it. "St. Michael gives me signs. With his guidance I believe we'll have the best chance of finding where they are."

* * *

Before noon I'm off to see my grandmam. The poison flakes, I have in a small container. The walk's a short one. When I reach her gate, I find it unlocked, which means she's been out early. I only hope that she's returned. I push the gate open and see her at the door to her small house. She waves to me.

"Lalin, I just came back from an early Mass," she calls. "How are you? It's been a while since you came by."

"Oh, Grandmam, you do forget. I was here only last week. We mixed some potions with your herbs. Don't you remember?"

"Hmm, if you say so, *mon cher*. What you got for me today?" She sees me pull the container from my pocket.

"Let's go inside," I say, "I need to explain some things about what's happened."

Her house is warm from a small fire, flickering in her parlor's fireplace. We sit at a table while I give her the details of all the problems from the day before. She's met Apolline and like me she's learned to trust her.

"Ah, a strange story, indeed. Let me have a look at this poison from the creature. You say it most looked like a spider."

"Since it disappeared before I could examine its remains, it's hard to describe exactly. I'm sure it had at least eight legs. It was hairy and larger than my hand. In fact, I would say more like two hands."

Grandmam's nose twitches like a rabbit. I almost laugh to see her make this face. "Let me take a closer look at this," she says. " Then she opens a box that sits in the middle of her table, takes out a clean, white cloth and a pair of tweezers. She takes my container and spreads the dark flakes on the cloth. With a small magnifying glass in hand, she leans across the cloth, bending to get a closer look.

At first, she says nothing, but then with the tweezers she captures one or two flakes, lifting them to her nose. "Ah ha," she whispers, "we have something like belladonna. It's certainly a strong, strong venom. I believe this was some supernatural creature. Not an ordinary spider."

"Yes, that was my thought too. I've never seen an insect so large."

Grandmam taps the tweezers against the wooden table. "Could it have been a bat then? A bite from a strange bat could be quite a danger."

"No, no, no," I lean closer to her, "this creature had many legs I've told you. No bat looks like that. Plus, it didn't fly. It crawled."

"This thing that you describe reminds me of a legend I once heard." Her eyes go narrow as she speaks. "A creature called Arachne with many features like a spider, but much larger than what you describe. Their bite could make the victim become like them."

"*Mon Dieu*, that story gives me such a chill." I feel the goose bumps pop up on my forearms. "I have to pray that it was not that creature."

Grandmam shakes her head. "I can't tell you what the poison is, but I will make a tincture with these flakes and that might tell us more."

"Thank you for your trouble," I say and give her a strong hug and a kiss against her cheek. "We'll meet again soon, but now I must check on Apolline and make sure she's feeling no more effect from that bite."

* * *

Grandmam's story of the Arachne legend gives me new fears. I walk fast along the banquette. To the market I must hurry to find Apolline. If she's recovered, she would be there by now, setting up her table with charms and potions to sell.

Many people brush pass me as I go. A cold wind gusts round the corners of the buildings. Clouds have drifted across the sky and the day grows gray. A few raindrops begin to fall. I see some vendors covering their wares. Well-dressed gentlemen stop to open their umbrellas. Already I am rushing by our cathedral and crossing to the Place d'Armes. One more corner to turn before I reach the marketplace.

At the market I pause to take a deep breath and look around. Many sellers work at setting up their tables. The roof here keeps them covered from the raindrops. Someone's laid out fresh flowers. The fragrance floats nearby. Apolline's not in her usual place, and this worries me. I wander about between the vendor stands. One woman calls to me. Ah, I recognize her; she often comes to my bayou meetings where I give her some good potions and she always pays me well for them.

"Mamzelle Lalin," she says as I approach her table spread with charms, candles, and lovely pictures of our saints. "It's a surprise to see you here among these vendors stands. You're the Queen of all our magic arts. You have no need for these wares I'm sure."

I smile at her. "It's true I'm not here to shop today," I say. "I'm looking for a friend, Apolline Carriere. Do you know her?"

"Yes, I do know Apolline. She's not been around today. Someone said she's not feeling well."

My stomach sinks a bit when she says this. "Who saw her this day?"

The woman turns to a mulatto man who's setting out some bottles on a bench next to her. "Marcel, don't you live near Apolline Carriere? Did you see her this morning?"

"Yes, she stays in a cabin right behind me. I saw her step out on her porch before I left. I ask her if she needed me to carry her to town in my wagon. But she said that she's recovering from a sickness and needed to rest for the day."

"How did she look? I'm wondering if I need to go and check on her."

"Well, she say that she had a spider bite her, but then she say the strangest thing." He walks over to us, hesitates, and speaking softly says. "She told me that she couldn't sleep for the whole night. Bad dreams haunt her. In these nightmares she saw herself sprouting hairy legs and crawling on the floor like some ugly bug."

The woman standing next to me gasps and presses one hand against her lips. "What an awful thing to dream, poor Apolline!"

"But how did she look to you this morning?" I ask again.

He blows a puff of air between his lips and shrugs. "Well, her eyes were very red from lack of sleep, but otherwise she looked herself."

I take a sigh of relief, remembering that I was most careful to remove all the poison from her wound. Still a chill creeps up my spine. Could it be a creature like the Arachne that my grandmam described that stung her? And, if that's true, I only pray that my treatment left nothing of the venom inside her body.

The man, Marcel, turns to me. "If you come back late afternoon, I can ride you there in my wagon, so you can check on her."

I thank him for his kind offer and tell him I'll return, if I decide to go. The afternoon is young still. I need time to think this through. If I return to my house on Burgundy, I can make an offering to my saints. I feel my Erzulie will give her best advice this day.

Chapter Ten

A drizzling rain falls as I hurry, walking fast to reach my house. While I rush down one alley, I hear a carriage pull up behind me and turn to see. A surprise, it is, to see my Etienne. What luck that he's on his way to join me for a midday meal. He jumps down from his driver's seat to help me climb up beside him. I see some passersby give us a long look. His behavior has crossed some boundaries. Even though most young Creole men have their quadroon mistresses, it's not permissible to be seen with them on the city streets in broad daylight. Still Etienne lost his wife, so these folks can only make reports to his family.

I hold my head high as we roll through the streets, making sure my tignon's tied tight around my head, concealing my long dark hair. As we travel, I tell him what my grandmam told me this morning and what I just heard at the market about Apolline.

He reins in the horses to make the turn onto Rue Burgundy. "Are you on your way to check on her?" he asks.

"It's much too far to walk, Etienne. I was on my way to make an offering to my saints. If they favor me today, I get an answer to the problem."

"I called a carriage for her once but didn't ride with her to her cabin. I told the driver to make sure for her safety. She lives far out of town I think."

"At the market they told me where I would find her if she's at home. It's some few miles from here on the last alleyway before the bayou road."

We reach my house, and he slows the carriage to a halt, turning to me with a question. "If you only want to check on her well-being, I can steer my horses in that direction. I have one hour before a meeting at my office."

"No matter what we find, I won't keep you. I can stay with her. *Merci, merci*, let's go."

He slaps the reins against the horse's hinds, and we continue down Rue Burgundy. At the next corner we turn and roll on through the city until we reach the outskirts.

I've made a mental note of the roads that Marcel mentioned. Neighborhoods grow shabby as we ride into this area. Small houses crowd together on weed-filled land pockets. Some of these are well-kept with pastel shaded walls, but others have broken windows and peeling paint.

"Turn here," I say, "I'm sure this must be the place."

Etienne steers the carriage as I direct him. A bumpy road, this is, with deep ruts and fallen branches strewn about the sides. We pass a few gray cabins spaced out between some straggly oaks.

"I think she's there." I point at a tiny shack that stands behind one small shotgun house.

When he slows to a stop, I hop out. "Wait here," I call back to him.

"There may be danger." He jumps down from his driver's seat, leaving the carriage in the middle of the dirt road.

Together we climb up wooden steps and approach the door. I tap against the boards. Inside someone groans softly.

"Apolline, it's me, Lalin, come to see how you are."

The sound of stocking feet shuffles to the door. Etienne grabs my arm and pulls me back behind himself, as the door creaks open. But it is indeed Apolline Carriere who stands before us. A loosely woven shawl she has wrapped around her body. Her eyes are streaked with webs of red veins.

"*Bonne amie*, you're ill. What's wrong?"

She shakes her head, rubs her eyes with one hand and then pulls back the shawl. It's the wound, the creature's bite, that she shows us. Some dark hairs and tendrils sprout from the spot that I treated only yesterday.

"It's eating at me, Mamzelle. This thing eats at my arm."

I move close to have a better look, and just then Etienne grips my shoulder and pulls me back. "Wait, Lalin, stand back. Let me have a look."

He takes me by surprise. "Are you a better judge than me?" I ask.

I can't believe how hard he grabs my shoulder and leans forward to have a closer look. When she makes a sudden move with her arm, he jumps back. Ah, now I understand. He recalls what Grandmam Selene told me and thinks Apolline may be taking on a new shape. He imagines the Arachne.

Apolline looks at me with wide eyes. It's puzzlement I think she feels.

"It's safe for me in any case, Etienne," I say. "I have my amulet. St. Michael will protect me."

"Lalin, someday your faith will betray you. Your amulet can't always save you."

At last I convince him to release me so I can have a close look. I do take care not to touch her arm with my bare hands. Clearly some venom remains there, but I think she can be healed.

"Apolline, you must gather up a change of clothes and anything you need from your cabin. We'll take you back to my house on Rue Burgundy. You require some treatment and a complete cleansing. And it's important for you stay with me for a few days."

✷ ✷ ✷

Within a half an hour we're at my house again. After much talk on the ride, I managed to assure Etienne that Apolline brings no danger. He sees she's fearful and suffers from some sharp pains around her wound. The redness spreads in streaks from the center of her sore, and the swelling is most alarming. I take a handkerchief from his pocket and give it to her. She wipes her eyes and thanks me for my kindness.

"*Mon cher,* I'll be back, as soon as the workday's ended," Etienne tells me. He still looks worried, but, after helping us down from the carriage seats, he takes the reins again and heads back to his office near the river.

Once we get inside, I tell Apolline what I must do to save her arm. First, she needs to drink the tea I make from sweet birch leaves. This tea will give relief from pain. Also birch bark I'll use to place against her skin. Some tinctures, I apply, made from the chili peppers that I keep with my supply of herbs. With the treatments I believe she will be cured.

When evening comes, I spend time with my love, while Apolline falls into a slumber on my chaise longue. All herbs, she took with the tea. Her fever dropped. The pain too left her free to have some soup before she fell asleep. If her progress continues, we'll know we saved her from this monster.

✷ ✷ ✷

When I wake there's flaxen light spilling through the drapes, spreading stripes across my boudoir floor. Etienne turns his head toward me on the pillow, but his eyes are still closed. He makes a long sigh in his sleep, and I wonder what he's dreaming.

I leave him to enjoy another hour of rest before the day begins. Sliding off the side of my four-posted bed, I slip on a dressing gown and head through the short hall to my parlor to check on Apolline.

Looking through the archway into the parlor, I see she's gone. No sign of her in the room. I continue through the French doors that open onto my courtyard. The air's still heavy with moisture from some evening showers. The sun barely streams its early beams across my neighbor's roof and through the upper branches of my oak tree.

I whisper words inside my head. Where could she be? Surely, she would not leave me in the middle of the night without a word. She might be in the kitchen room. Across my small courtyard I see now that the door to that room is open. But as I come near, my Erzulie flashes in my head. A warning she sends me that my friend's not well.

The room's dark except for bands of light that stream in through one window. Peering through the open door, I can see the storage cupboards and my cooking stove. No one's in the room. I step inside, so my eyes may adjust to this dim light. Something like a pile of clothes or towels lies in one corner near to one side of my stove. I push the door open wider to let more light inside, and I see the pile of cloth move out of the corner and across the floor. Stumbling back, I fall against the door. What is this?

"Erzulie, no!" I cry, when I see that the pile of clothes is my friend, Apolline. I see her face and hear her moan, but it seems she has two extra arms or maybe more. Her limbs have turned dark and spindly. She tries to pull herself up off the floor, but instead of rising, she can only skittle closer to me on her stomach.

My body freezes. I can't think what to do. I reach quickly for my amulet, hanging round my neck, hidden inside the folds of this silk dressing gown.

Chapter Eleven

My first thought is to get to Grandmam. If anyone can help my friend, it will be her.

Apolline struggles with her hairy, bony limbs. She tries to speak but her words come out in low pitched groans. There's one spindle backed chair in a corner by the cupboards.

"Here let me help you get up off the cold floor," I say to her. She croaks some harsh sounds, as I approach.

"Let's try to get you in the chair." I push it across the floor toward her. As I get closer, I can see her legs have turned a dark metallic color. Her head and body appear smaller. There's a kind of sheen reflected off her arms and legs. I reach for her hands. "Oh no," I whisper," her hands have shriveled at the end of her appendages. Long and thin, these arms and legs splay out around her body.

I grab two of her arms to pull her off the floor. With luck I'm able to drag her to the chair where I can plop her on the seat. Nearly toppling over from the weight, I catch my balance. I take one deep breath before I speak to her again.

"Can you drink something? Some water?" I ask. She shakes her head. Her eyes are wet now with tears.

"We will find a way to stop this thing." My lips feel dry and taut. I can't make a smile. "Try to stay as calm as you can, while I go to my grandmam. Between the two of us, we'll find a way to break this spell."

Her eyes are round, unblinking. I reach to stroke her for a moment before I head out the door. Across my courtyard, I run and through the parlor to the bedroom, where I throw on a blouse and tie my full, blue skirt around my waist. I wish I could let Etienne know what has happened, but there's no time for that.

Within some few minutes, I am out my front door. Up the street I hurry to Grandmam Selene, almost running on the banquette. The heel on one shoe catches on the walkway edge; I stagger nearly falling onto the hard surface. One more block I chant to myself, as I turn the corner onto Rue St. Ann.

Grandmam surely hears her gate slam as I run through. I give her a quick story of what has happened with Apolline.

Her face looks sad; she reaches for my hand. Hugging me, she says, "Ah, I do know a spell for this one. It may look bad, but I have my ways." she says. "Let me bring some things with me."

I help her find the candles that she needs. The other supplies I will have at my house she says and off we go. It's not worth the time to hail a carriage. Even at her age Grandmam Selene takes a fast stride with me, as we hurry along Rue Burgundy. In some few minutes we reach the house. We push through my louvered door, through the front rooms and out the French doors to the courtyard and the kitchen room.

When she sees Apolline cowering on the stool where I have left her, my grandmam goes to her quickly and whispers prayers. Without further hesitation she tells me to find a piece a chalk to draw a circle on the floor of the room.

She shakes a finger at me. "Quick-- get salt and one deep bowl. Fill the bowl to the top with water."

While I find these things, she takes one red candle and a black one from her cloth bag. She pulls at the wicks to stretch them long.

I bring a tall clay bowl brimming with the fresh water. A small bag of salt I place beside it. Now I watch as Grandmam places both candles in the bowl, so that they are almost covered with the water. Only the wick tips rise above the water. She lights both candles with a wooden match. We watch the flames flare up. The two of us have the strength to lift up Apolline and place her in the circle near the bowl. Her spidery legs and arms splay out around her.

"No time to waste, Lalin, sprinkle one handful of salt across the water in the bowl."

I follow what she tells me. And she speaks to the spirits while I listen. "Erzulie, bring your powers to this salt. Let the sparks be seen in this bowl."

As she speaks the words, I see the water lights up in the darkness of the room. Apolline rolls her wide eyes and moans, but then grows quiet looking at the shining liquid.

Grandmam sings out a chant. Her voice, high-pitched and tuneful, soars to the ceiling. Our candles flicker as the wax melts into the glowing surface.

"*Destroy the web that has been spun.*
the evil work a spider's done. Take the
harm away from this good woman, our Apolline."

I stand beside my grandmam while the candles burn down to the water's level. Energy from the salt glimmers in the liquid. Soon the candles sputter; they flare once more before the flame is gone.

"Wet your hands and sprinkle that salty energy onto Apolline," she says.

I dip my fingers in the bowl. With dripping hands, I fling drops on my friend. She shivers first, but then I see what begins to happen. The hair is dropping off her limbs. The skin slowly changes to a normal hue. Odd appendages begin to shrink.

"Take both candles from the water, Lalin. Hold them lengthwise across your chest."

I follow these directions, listening while Grandmam prays out to Erzulie.

"Reverse this evil spell, my precious lady! Return this woman to her rightful state."

Apolline's body slowly changes. Her torso comes to its normal size. Some time passes before she's back into herself. Her breathing falters here and there, but gradually she pulls herself up with Grandmam's help. She stands inside the circle, swaying side to side. I move to her so that she can lean on me.

"You must break the candles, Lalin, first in half and then in small pieces. It's time to pour half the salty water over these wax remains. We'll bury the candle pieces in your courtyard flower bed." Grandmam rubs my shoulder, leads me through the kitchen room and out into the courtyard. "The final way to break this spell will be to pour the sparkling energy on the burial mound."

This last step I follow closely. We help my friend regain her balance. Her face relaxes. She rubs her arms, then bends to touch her legs.

"*Bondye*, bless you both. I'm well again." She smiles at us. Her eyes bright with happiness and relief.

✱ ✱ ✱

What a day this has been! We clean up from the candle spell. After giving more prayers to our saints, we help Apolline to get steady on her feet again. She rests now on my chaise longue in the parlor. Grandmam sits on the sofa while I make tea. We sip from our china cups in silence.

Grandmam assures me that she feels fine to walk home on her own. One long hug I give her and many thanks before she leaves. Before she goes, she tells me, "You and Apolline must make a pretty offering to the saints for all this help they've offered us this day."

✱ ✱ ✱

At evening I describe the events to Etienne, while he pours himself a second glass of wine. He sighs and stares at me. "The horrors that come from all this voudou magic make me angry, Lalin. The evil aspects of the sorcery bring danger. " He takes a long drink from his stemmed glass. "Think of all the grief that happened with the loup garou. Now we have a spider spell, and who knows what may rise or fall from the sky tomorrow."

I lick my lips, taking one deep breath before I answer him. "Yes, yes, I can understand how you feel. It's been a frightening time, but we came through it. Can't you be happy that Apolline's free from the Arachne spell?"

He starts to shake a finger at me, but then he hesitates, puts his glass down on the table, bites his lower lip and walks across the room to take me in his arms. I melt into his chest, tears forming at the corners of my eyes. "*Mon ange*," he says, "it's because I love you that I have to take these firm stands. Please, stay with your healing rites. But you must avoid all evil sources."

With my arms circled around his neck I give him one long kiss, pressing my lips hard against his. We linger in this embrace. His tension eases with the passion that we share now. Soon he lifts me off my feet. What happens then, I can only say brings all the pleasure I can allow myself. Angry words are buried in one blissful hour in my boudoir, while Apolline sleeps peacefully in my parlor.

Chapter Twelve

    This afternoon I prepare a fine seafood gumbo for Etienne. I add fresh shrimp and okra from our market. While it's cooking on my stove, I go out into the courtyard to make a candle circle. Apolline will create offerings at her cabin near the bayou road. She stopped by to give me one beautiful picture of St. Michael. He looks the same as on my holy amulet. Only this likeness is painted on a card with his tunic in shades of red and blue. His sword is drawn, pointing at the evil one, who lies beneath him on the ground.

    The picture I place in the center of the circle. Soon I ladle a portion of the spicy gumbo into a bowl for my saint. He also likes cinnamon and rosemary. These I blend into an oil to offer him. My red candles are lit. I sing my prayer and with it I rise on my toes. swaying, bending. With swirling turns, I circle all the candles and feel Erzulie take control. She has St. Michael as her guardian. He protects her before all others, and she's grateful for his attention to her wellbeing.

    The courtyard garden fades around me. Sinking to the stone, I have a vision of the woods, where I find I'm standing near the bayou. As I weave my way between the trees, I get a breath of honeysuckle. That sweet fragrance lures me on. Logs and broken limbs are everywhere. I have my sandals on, so I won't get cuts and bruises on my feet. Sunlight streams through the oak leaves making yellow ribbons and lacey patterns between the shadows of the trees. What a lovely scene! I wonder what it means. But then I stop short almost by an instinct to listen to a sound of horse's hooves pounding on a road.

    The forest breaks onto a wide dirt trail. Clomping hooves sound closer, so I pause behind one giant oak. Dust flies, making quite a cloud to hide this horseman. While I wait to catch a glimpse of him, a flock of quail flutters through the oaks then skitters back into surrounding swamplands.

A great black stallion emerges from the cloud. At first its head appears, mane flying in the breeze. Neighing sounds vibrate in the air. Then I see the man. The wind lifts his dark cloak and reveals his black waistcoat. His top hat pulled down to his ears, stays in place even with the speed he travels.

What a sight he is as he reins in his horse and comes near my hiding place. My heart tumbles like a small animal in my chest, but I make no sound. A full stop he makes. He looks around. His horse prances in a nervous circle. He's a white Creole man of middle age. His hair's dark but streaked with gray at his temples. His face is sternly handsome. I stare now at his eyebrows, peaking under the top hat brim. Do they meet as one above his nose? I'm not quite sure

Does he know I'm here behind this big tree? A voice in my head tells me to step out and make my presence known. Still I hesitate and try to hear some message from my saints, but there's no answer. A swirling breeze comes up around me, and I'm pulled or pushed out from my hiding place. How this happens, I can't be sure.

I face him, standing in the middle of the trail. Ah, his lips spread into the most amazing smile. The stallion neighs again and rears up on its hind legs. For a moment I think I will be trampled by this beast, but he manages to calm the animal. It shakes its mane, while he whispers some soothing words. Again, he grins at me. Deep lines surround his eyes. He's clearly an older fellow.

"Monsieur," I say to him, "I'm lost and must get back to town." I think, if he feels some sympathy for me, I may be safe with him.

He doesn't speak but lifts one gloved hand and beacons me to come to him.

I feel the wind spinning all around me. Icy cold it draws me in to it. I struggle to control the pull. How strange to wrestle with the wind. The image blurs, and I find myself lying on the stones of my own courtyard.

This vision leaves me shaking. I will meet this man sometime soon; that's one thing I know for certain. But the meaning of the dream doesn't come to me. I pray St. Michael will choose to give me answers.

Chapter Thirteen

We make our plans at last. Tonight, Etienne and I will venture out to discover what we can at the cottage near Bayou St. John. When I describe my vision to him, he frowns then sighs. I wait for him to speak, but he says nothing.

"It's good at least you make no remarks," I say to him. "We'll see what we will see, and I fear this horseman will appear."

"Are you ready then?" he asks and wraps one arm around my waist while I'm trying to adjust my shawl.

"It's not the time for cuddles, love. We face some dangers."

"I know, Lalin." He nods, withdraws his arm and stares at me. I think he's pouting. "I would in fact prefer that you stay home and let me have a look at this place alone. When I return, I can tell what I've seen."

"Oh no, we go together. We shapeshift and spy on the loup garou and their sweet Yvette. Besides," and now I do smile at him, "that girl is after you for better or for worse. We don't know, if she still wants to marry you or she wishes to take revenge for your desertion."

He ignores my comments on Yvette. "Well, I plan for you to stay back among the trees, so that you can make a quick escape in case there's a problem."

I do sigh and take one long breath. "I know that it's hard for you to understand, but I have to see all I can about them and what is going on. All the information helps me understand what I must do next. You never fully accept that my powers from the saints will protect me. And where's your gold cross?" I reach one hand down his shirt. "Ah, yes, at least you do have it on. Please, please never take it off."

He nods, grabs his hat from the rack and says, "It's time, Lalin. No more talk. We go!"

Outside he's parked his carriage at the corner of Dumaine. I lock my door behind us, and we are off.

Once we reach the bayou road, we find it covered with a heavy fog. Etienne slows his carriage, reining in the horses, speaking to them softly.

"This mist is like a cloud tonight. We'd best tie up here and go ahead on foot. We can't be too far from that little hut." He turns to me to see if I agree.

"As you wish, you do know best I'm sure."

He smiles at me and leans to kiss me softly on the lips. "Yes, but I suspect you have some vision in your head at this moment. The magic tells you that I am right this time."

Down he hops, to tie his horses to some skinny tree and leaves the beasts some water. We both make sure to button up our cloaks as the evening has become a chilly night.

Before we begin our hike, Etienne says, "I think we should wait to shift our shapes. We can travel faster in our human forms, and with our height we'll see better what's ahead."

I nod. It's true that we can spot things in the distance better with our height, but for speed my feline self can scamper faster through the brush. "We'll wait then," I agree.

For some time, we travel along the road, passing no one. This night is so black that I fear that once we cut into the woods without a trail to follow, we'll be tripping, falling over branches, stumps and end up with cuts and bruises at the best.

Maybe half an hour later Etienne raises up his hand and stops. When I start to speak, he puts his hand across my lips. Did he hear something that I missed? Just then a doe almost rushes head on into us. She leaps in the air; a fawn stands frozen on one side. They pause there for seconds and then bound off across the road, disappearing into the fog.

Etienne whispers to me, "I think we're getting close. We need your magic to give us our feline shapes, Lalin."

I pray for a quick shapeshift. When nothing happens for several minutes, Etienne shrugs and widens eyes at me. St. Michael takes his time tonight. I dig into my pockets to find a bag of gris-gris. With these herbs in my hand, I pray again. Something flutters around my head. A bat circles. Is this a sign? I take a handful of my powders, toss them in the air above my head and throw some over Etienne. He shudders, but the charm begins to work. He falls to the ground. His body starts to shrink. Feet and hands changing into paws. Soon my ginger tabby has his fur and bushy tail.

"Holy mother, hear my prayer," I whisper. Finally, I am sinking to the ground. I sigh in relief, as my transformation comes.

We're ready to continue through the woods. I am thankful for my cat eyes tonight. The sky's so dark with clouds that I fear we'd be lost without our keen night vision.

When at last we reach the clearing with the hut, the sight is disappointing. There's no light in the windows this night. I felt for certain that I had a clear message from my saints we'd find someone here this evening.

Etienne's golden eyes flash in the darkness. "Where are they?"

"I had word that they would be here. Perhaps we missed them."

We decide to wait. It seems an hour passes with insects buzzing in our ears. Lightening bugs flash like tiny stars around us. A snake or two slithers through the vines, and my ginger tabby claws one as it slides too close to him. My fur grows damp from the descending mist.

I growl, "There's some mistake. I can't explain it, but we should head back to the road. There's nothing here for us to see tonight."

Etienne growls in his throat, and we both swish our tails and wind our way back through the trees to reach the road. We need to make our change before we get to the carriage, so we stop along the road while I make entreaties to my saints.

When we both stand as ourselves again, I say, "Strange, it is, that we found no one at the cottage. Somehow my senses failed me."

"Well, only one wasted evening." And, as he says these words, the sound of hooves breaks the silence. At a distance from us, but quite distinct. Etienne turns wide eyes to me. "Who's riding on this road in the middle of the night?" He picks up a thick piece of limb that lies near the edge of the road and tests the strength of it. I shiver in the damp air, listening to the sounds, clutching at the memory that travels in my head. Is it possible?

Chapter Fourteen

The fog grows denser, obscuring all but the largest of the oaks and cypress trees. The beating of the hooves against this road echoes in our ears, a steady rhythm that vibrates with such intensity that I feel my heart pick up the tempo. The pattern fills me. Etienne grabs my hand and pulls me to him, as if to shield me. We wait unmoving, as the horseman appears at a distance.

It's him. Yes, the strange rider from my vision gallops toward us. His pace slows as he approaches. His top hat's pulled tight around his ears. A cloak swirls around his body, lifted by a breeze. An elegant figure, he is. The stallion neighs, snorts and rears up on its hind legs. This fellow taps a riding whip against the horse's loins. The beast calms, as he strokes its long black mane. Etienne whispers to me that we'll stand our ground and meet this stranger face to face.

Ah, the smile that curls this fellow's lips, I remember that too, but this time he speaks, while we both stand there in the darkness. Etienne has one arm tight around my waist.

The impressive Creole gentleman speaks in a clear, deep voice. "What's this? A handsome couple along this lonely road so late at night. Have you lost your way? Where's your carriage?"

Hmm, I think to myself, perhaps this fellow's different. He doesn't look as frightening as the rider in my dream. He sounds almost concerned for us. I don't sense an evil presence, but he's imposing. Almost as handsome as my Etienne, but much, much older. He would be my father's age I'd say.

"Let me introduce myself," he says. "I am Lycus Volcain visiting in this country. I come from Arles in the south of France."

Etienne still holds me as he introduces himself, and describes me as his *femme*, Lalin. Monsieur Volcain tips his hat to me. It's then that I can see his eyebrows, dark and bushy. Indeed, they almost meet above his nose, but not quite. Quickly I avert my eyes, as I see he notes my stare.

"I expect you find my appearance as surprising as I find yours." His eyes grow narrow, but then he flashes his engaging smile. "It happens that I have friends living near the road and found that they are not at home tonight, so was on my way back to the city."

He looks at Etienne, and I suspect that he expects some explanation for our presence here in the middle of the night.

"Yes, well, it seems we have made a mistake as well. We planned to visit friends but took a wrong turn. Some strange animal spooked our horses back there." Etienne turns and points in the direction of where he has the animals tied to a tree. "We walked away to make sure the beast wasn't lurking about." He gestures to the stick he's dropped beside the road. "I grabbed a limb to have some defense."

"Hmm, yes, I saw you ready to defend yourself." The smile floods his face again, but this time Monsieur Volcain pulls something from his pocket. As he does this, I feel my Etienne pull me slightly back.

It's not a weapon that he takes out, but a card. He swings down from his saddle and presents his card to us with a bow and flourish of his top hat. Just as quick he stands up tall. He's a little taller than my Etienne.

We stare down at the stiff paper that describes his identity. This information looks impressive. He claims a medical license from a university in France, and a dukedom in the south as well. I glance up to see him purse his lips, as he waits for some reaction.

"So, Monsieur, are you addressed as a doctor or a count. Which title is most appropriate?" Etienne holds out the card, as if to return it.

To my surprise this man laughs out loud. He gestures for Etienne to keep his card. "My titles mean nothing in this city. My business here is to study herbal remedies that are used around this area. I record them for my book."

His eyes fall on me now. I'm sure of it, although he quickly averts them back to Etienne. My heart beats a faster rhythm, and I wait for Etienne to speak.

"Is your study here in the city?"

I watch my protector's face now, as he speaks. He drops the card into his waistcoat pocket, taps a finger against his lips, smiles at me and then continues speaking directly to the gentleman.

"Herbal remedies are associated with the voudou cult in this region, Monsieur. I'm sure you must be aware of that. Some folks fear these concoctions while others, of course, swear by the healing they perform. In any case, it's a pleasure to meet you even under these odd circumstances." Etienne pulls his own card from his vest pocket and hands it to Monsieur Volcain.

"Ah, a shipping business, I see. I'm delighted to meet you too and your *femme*."

"Perhaps we'll meet again then. We must find our carriage and head back to the Quarter in the city." Etienne bows slightly, and we take our leave.

As this impressive Frenchman remounts his horse, he calls out to us, "I will indeed look forward to our next meeting, Monsieur Legendre." And he taps his stallion with the riding whip and gallops off, dust flying behind him until he disappears into darkness.

✼ ✼ ✼

Although Etienne and I have some brief discussion about our encounter with Lycus Volcain, I am so exhausted from our running in the woods that I fall asleep in the carriage on the return ride to the city. Waking drowsy when we reach my house on Burgundy, I go straight to my boudoir, where I crawl into my canopy bed without even washing up.

When I wake in the morning, Etienne sleeps soundly by my side, making just the slightest snoring noise as he turns over on his side. My thoughts immediately return to our evening in the bayou woods. Sadly, nothing was accomplished. We never saw our enemies. We still know nothing of them since our trip there some weeks ago. My saints misled me, and that, I must say, rarely happens. I missed something in the vision. Before we set out on our adventure, I had seen the lighted house. I admit the human images were willowy and vague more like shadows than human figures, but a presence was clearly indicated. Strange, I think to myself.

And then to make the night more unpredictable than ever, my vision of the elegant rider came to reality. Could this man have some connection to the loup garou? Why did he appear frightening in the dream? It seemed a warning, but from what I saw last night he seemed more impressive than alarming.

As soon as, Etienne has his breakfast I will make an offering, light candles, and pray to my St. Michael. I decide to quickly dress for the day and brew the coffee in my kitchen room. From my armoire I pull out a peach-colored cotton skirt and one of my white blouses, run a quick comb through my hair and dab on a drop or two of the French perfume that my love gifted me.

When I come back through the French doors after brewing coffee, I see that Etienne is up and dressed for the day.

"Good morning, love," he says. His smile never fails to thrill me.

"And a lovely morning to you, *mon cher*." I pour his coffee from my pot and add the hot milk, handing him a full cup.

He takes a sip and places the cup on the table. He beckons me to come to him for an embrace. My body always fills with such excitement when we come together. Our lips press tight in our kiss then soften as we step apart. As lovely as he feels against me, I know that he must take his leave. We will have our love later.

I pour myself a cup of cafe and watch him as he sips his. The images of last evening return to me and I decide to ask. "What did you think of our encounter with Monsieur Volcain?" I hesitate to remind him about my vision.

"Hmm, yes, it was a strange meeting. Odd, indeed, Lalin. I have an idea to try to find out more about him. Learn, if he's known in the city. I've never seen or heard of him before last night." He pulls the calling card out of his waistcoat pocket and stares down at it. "Duke de Languedoc. Surely he has friends or family in the city."

CHAPTER FIFTEEN

Nearly two weeks pass before we hear news of Lycus Volcain, although my protector has inquired of many in our Vieux Carre. I too have asked at the market and spoken to my followers about this man. It seems that no one's heard of him. Our enemies, the trio of them, have also been in hiding or so it seems.

Then one evening Etienne comes to me in an excited state. He tells me that he finally did hear word of the mysterious horseman from France.

"An old customer of Papa's from the plantation, Magnolia's Rose, stopped by the office this afternoon. He said that he'd had a recent visitor at his home there. He described an elegant fellow, a medical doctor, from the south of France. My ears perked when I heard that."

"Lycus Volcain? Was it really the same?" I ask.

"It's true," he says, turning to face me as he hangs his coat on the rack. "We compared the calling cards." He winks at me as he pulls the same card from his pants pocket.

"Tell me; tell me. What did the customer say?"

Etienne pulls something else from his pocket. It appears to be a column from a local paper. He hands it to me, pointing at some words that have been underlined. Then I see the name.

This week a famous doctor came to visit Monsieur Babineaux at Magnolia's Rose. This medical man, Lycus Volcain, arrived in New Orleans only recently from the south of France. He is a distant cousin of the family, who had not heard from him in many years. Monsieur and Madame Babineaux entertained their guest with a soiree, inviting many of their friends from surrounding plantations. This illustrious gentleman will meet with local folk to research for a book that he plans to write on herbal remedies. He states that meeting with local voudou folks may be of interest to him.

"Hmm, so the Monsieur Babineaux is a customer of yours?" I ask.

"That's right, but it's what came next that truly did amaze me. Papa was meeting with another customer in his main office, so I was left alone with this plantation owner." Etienne lowers his voice to near a whisper. "A shock he gave me, Lalin. He asked me about you."

"What? How could he know about me?"

"First the gentleman claims he's heard about the case of Minette's strange death, and how the police pursued me." Etienne presses one finger against his lips, hesitating before he speaks again. "But then the man said that the word's spread that my *placée*, my octoroon mistress, is a priestess, a well-known healer. Many folks from the city and along the bayous know your reputation."

"Well, of course, my followers know who I am. No one doubts that, so what else?"

"I felt that he had no business to ask me about you, Lalin. I let him know that I didn't wish to share my private life. He shrugged and said that he only thought it would be of interest to his cousin, who had a mission to collect and study herbal remedies."

I shake my head. Thoughts crowd my mind, and I feel a calling to consult my saints. "For certain, we have not seen the last of Lycus Volcain," I say. "He seems a mystery to me. I've no clear sense of his motives."

* * *

My plans to make an offering to St. Michael have been delayed. One day after my conversation with my protector, I learn that he must make a business trip by riverboat. He needs to meet with a potential customer, who has a large plantation further north. Since he may be gone for some weeks, he wants to spend more time with me before he leaves.

We spend three whole days and nights together, leaving my boudoir for only a few hours here and there to take a meal. Once we have a carriage ride along the river road to a secluded place that Etienne discovers. There we share some wine and a quiet meal. With our stomachs full, we lay together on a quilt and make love beneath the giant oaks.

When at last we have enjoyed all our passion on this lovely afternoon, we both stretch out to rest. I'm still entangled in his embrace even as he closes his eyes, breaths deeply and falls asleep. Wriggling free of his strong arms, I sit up to take in this scene along the levee. The river drifts below us, growing wider in the distance. One paddle wheeler travels through the muddy waters, churning, churning against the current. A flock of great white birds skims along near the surface of the rippling river. Egrets, I think, but of that I can't be sure.

The sun still shines above the horizon. A line of puffy clouds borders treetops that rise across the river's winding way. I look down at my Etienne and admire his manly beauty. His shirt and pants unbuttoned still. The fine muscles of his chest, his smooth skin are enough to give me tiny goose bumps along my own skin. I want to touch him, but not to wake him. Smiling to myself, I decide to lay back on our quilt, not to sleep, but just to give some thought to events of recent weeks.

When I close my eyes, I hear a voice whisper in my head. It happens sometimes that out of nowhere St. Michael comes to me. He gives no warning. Now he shows me scenes. I see Appolline Carriere walking on the banquette near my house on Rue Burgundy. Who's with her? A shadow moves by her side, but I can't make out the form. I pray to have a clearer picture, but then the scene changes, and I see the market.

I'm amazed as I gaze all around the many stalls. It feels so real that I could touch the fruits and vegetables displayed on make-shift tables. Ah, the sweet smell of cakes drifts to my nose. Only few vendors sit on boxes or stand behind their stalls. There's no sound and very little movement in this vision.

The scene is quiet and restful, and I decide to wait to see what my Saint wants to show me here. I know he has a message, if I am patient and wait, the meaning will come to me. Then I see the man. He comes strolling with his top hat pulled tight above his ears. He wears his cape; his riding boots hug his long legs. Meandering between the many stalls, he nods at these vendors. His lips move, but I hear no words.

Then I see her. It's Appolline again. She sits on a stool behind her table. Her wares spread across the surface. There are roots, some powders, and bags of gris-gris. Pictures of the saints are displayed on one side of her stand. In a flash, Monsieur Volcain appears right in front of her. My breath catches in my throat. What's happening here? I pray this vision doesn't float away.

They talk now. If only I could hear the words. He points to several bags of gris-gris. Apolline picks one out and holds it out to him. She also shows him herbs and roots that I recognize. These are ones that I have taught her how to use. I can't discern from her expressions whether she knows this man. I sense that he's a stranger to her, but I can't be sure. Next, he gives her his calling card. He takes out a pen and writes something on the back. If I could only move in closer, I could see the words.

He reaches in his pocket once more, pulls out some coins and purchases several bags of gris-gris along with bags of herbs and roots. Now I follow him as he buys more herbs from another vendor. He browses at a stand that offers statues of the saints and candles. He talks with the seller, but then buys nothing.

On the banquette again, another vision forms. He's rapping on the door of one fine house on Rue Royal. This house looks familiar. Do I know this house or its owner? The door swings open.

Mon Dieu, I can't see who stands there on the other side. The open door has blocked my view. Monsieur Volcain walks through the entrance, and I see nothing. The door closes behind him. I shake my head and press my lips together.

The next thing I know, someone's shaking me by my shoulders. My eyes pop open. My Etienne. I'd drifted off to sleep he tells me.

"You were talking in your sleep," he says to me. "Mumbling so I could only catch a word or two. Sounded like you said, 'Let me see, let me see.' You even reached out with your hand."

I almost laugh when he tells me this, remembering that last scene in the open door. In the end I'm not quite sure whether I had a true vision or just a dream.

Chapter Sixteen

Etienne has left for his trip up the river. So today, I feel sad, but, if I keep busy with my healing work, my spirits stay higher.

I go to visit Grandmam Selene this morning. Wrap my hair in a tignon, wear my full blue skirt and a yellow blouse with long sleeves. A shawl will keep my shoulders warm enough. The winter's turning into spring.

It's a short walk to Grandmam's house. A few wagons filled with large baskets rumble down the road to market. At the corner of St. Ann near her house, a bantam rooster struts along the banquette. He picks up his speed when he sees me. Must think I'm out to catch him, but I stop at Grandmam's gate, while he swaggers on his way toward Rue Rampart. I wonder if his owner will find him this day.

Grandmam Selene is sweeping off her stoop this morning. She props her broom against the door when she sees me. We embrace and peck kisses on each other's cheeks.

"I came to pay a visit. I missed you at Mass on Sunday, so I come to check on you, and hear the latest news about our quarter."

She nods. "I knew you'd be by today, so I have a full pot of coffee and rolls to share with you."

Inside she sits at her dining table where she's set out cups and plates, as if she did know I was coming. "There is some news," she says. "The word's out that the Papa Lamba and your Tante Corinne are due to come to trial next month."

I pull up a chair to join her at the table. "I believe our city police have the evidence they need. With the devil's weed that they found and the fact that it matched with the poisons that were discovered in the victim's boudoir."

"They have enough to prove their guilt. Along with the attack they made on you and Etienne at that house on Esplanade. They're responsible for Etienne's wife Minette's death. And I still have the remedies laced with poisons that Corinne gave me, so that she could take control of me and my property." Grandmam takes a sip of coffee.

" I don't see any way they could avoid conviction. I wonder if we'll all be called as witness."

She sits back and rubs her chin. "It's certain that they will call upon you and Etienne when the time comes."

I must remember to give this news to Etienne too, although he may already know by the time he returns. We need to find out the court dates and whether there will be a jury for the trial.

I'm also thinking to ask Grandmam Selene if she has heard anything of our Monsieur Volcain. I've not done much traveling in my feline form around the Quarter in recent weeks, so don't know much of what's going on. She talks to folks at the market, and her older friends collect rumors as a hobby. Someone must have mentioned this distinguished gentleman.

"Grandmam, Etienne and I met a stranger in the city of late. Have you seen or heard of Monsieur Lycus Volcain? A handsome older fellow, tall and well dressed with fine credentials. The word is that he's a medical doctor and holds a dukedom or something like that in France."

She nods her head, blinks twice and folds her hands against her belly. "Hmm," she hums then says, "surprising that you have also met this person. Yes, he came to call on me just yesterday."

I gasp out loud. "How surprising! Whatever did he want with you? Did you let him in? What did he say?" My surprise is filled with fear for my grandmam's safety. What opinions I hold of this man are still in doubt.

"He claims, as you said, to be a doctor who's writing a book about the herb remedies we use in our healing practices. He showed me some credentials, which looked genuine and spoke as if he knows the plants and tinctures that we use. He made no mention of our saints or rituals."

"Yes, yes, but what did he ask of you?"

"In truth, he talked at length about his own knowledge and described some folks he met at one plantation along the river. In the end he pulled out a journal and showed me notes he'd made during his travels outside the city."

"And he asked you nothing about your own work?"

She clicks her tongue, hesitating. "He asked me if it was true that you had taken over for me at the bayou meetings. His exact words before we parted were, 'Could I meet with you again? And could you also have your granddaughter, Lalin Bonheur, here to join us?'

Me, I am not surprised by this last request. "So, tell me, please, what did you say then?"

"That I would have to speak to you before I could agree to such a meeting. But I had the sense that you would come by. The saints whispered in my ear you might say."

"It may be that I did have the inkling too. I'm not sure what to make of him. Twice I dreamed of him, but I can't be sure of the meaning of the dreams. " I hesitate before I tell the other thoughts I had about this man. "My first thought was that his eyebrows grew too close together."

"Ah, by the saints." Grandmam crosses herself quickly and grasps the gold medal she wears around her neck. "He has a slyness about him; it's true. Very charming this man is, but I noted nothing of the eyebrows, and his palms were free from hair."

"And yet you have the same feeling of caution about him that I feel. Should we make a prayer circle and ask for guidance from our good *Bondye*?"

"Yes, we both have doubt about meeting with him. If we consult our saints, make offerings, and pray for answers, we learn what to do about him."

✷ ✷ ✷

I have made my prayer circle and offered fine food and drink to our saints and our good God. No visions come to me. No answers to my questions appear. No messages from Grandmam Selene have come. So it is that when Monsieur Volcain contacts again, we will agree to meet.

Chapter Seventeen

Monsieur Volcain sent a message to Grandmam Selene. We now agree to meet this very evening. Both Grandmam and I prayed for answers, yet nothing came.

I did dream again of this fellow. In the picture that I saw, he was studying some leaves and flower petals with a microscope. He made notes as he changed the specimens. Nothing strange or sinister appeared in the image I had of him.

I also got a message from Etienne. He says his work takes longer than he thought. He'll be gone another week. I miss my love. Looking out now through my courtyard doors, I see the shadows spreading. Afternoon merges with the evening. It's time for me to dress for the meeting with Lycus Volcain.

* * *

I arrive early at Grandmam's house on St. Ann. She's brewing coffee, but I see that she's also fetched a fresh bottle of sherry. She's dressed in her best cotton skirt and blouse. Her long silver hair is twisted into a knot on top of her head. No need to scarf this evening, as we've no plans to leave her property.

Monsieur Volcain arrives late, striding through her gate with a swirling flourish of his black cape. Again, I am impressed with the elegance that this man exudes. He makes a slight bow to Grandmam and I, as he saunters through her open door without knocking.

"*Bon soir, Mesdames*," he says. "I have been very anxious for this meeting. It is such a pleasure to see you again, Madame Selene and Mademoiselle Lalin Bonheur."

"*Echante, Monsieur*." I extend my hand to him, and he dips his head to brush his lips against my fingers. This gesture I did not anticipate, but I do smile at him and nod.

Now he takes Grandmam's arm and leads her to the table. She has set it with her best wine glasses. The coffee pot and cups also rest on a tray at the other end.

We all sit at the table. She offers him a glass of sherry, which he accepts. For some minutes we share some small talk about his travels, and he listens while Grandmam describes her day of shopping at the market.

I decide then to pursue the purpose of his visit. "Monsieur, my Grandmam Selene asked me to come here tonight at your request. Perhaps I can learn something of your medical practice and why it is that you have this strong interest in our local healing methods."

"Mademoiselle Bonheur, may I call you Lalin. And please do call me Lycus or Dr. Lycus, as some prefer."

I smile again. "Yes, of course. But do tell us more about your practice."

He reaches in a pocket of his jacket and pulls out a small journal. "I have taken notes at a few plantations along the river and also inland when I traveled back into the bayou country." He opens the notebook, flips through some pages finally stopping when he finds the page he needs. "Let me show you things I discovered." He hands me the journal, pointing to a page.

Hmm, I think to myself. He's made notes on foxglove which grows wild sometimes outside the city. It makes a pretty purple flower but carries deadly poisons to animals and people. I look through several of his pages and see that he has listed other plants that bring sickness if they are eaten. He shows these notes, but, says nothing of his medical practice. Should I ask again? Perhaps I'll wait for now and pursue his interest in these unsafe plants.

"I see, Monsieur, you are making notes and descriptions of some plants that may be deadly if tasted by a person."

"Ah, so you are aware of these then?"

"Yes, but most have some useful purposes as well." I take a moment to read through these pages, and when I raise my head, I see he stares at me with narrowed eyes.

"Indeed," he says with a question in his voice.

"Yes, it's true. There's something in the foxglove that's good for people suffering with their heart. This remedy's not well known, but my saints have passed their wisdom on to us." I point to Grandmam too, as I say these words. "And belladonna also can be useful, if we are careful with its use."

He sniffs, and his nostrils flare. "How's that so? You use a poison to heal?"

"It's like this," Grandmam Selene chimes in, "it can help kill pain from joints or nerves."

Dr. Lycus clasps his hands together. "I'd like to see how these things work. In my notes I have them classed as poisonous. To be avoided."

I turn to Grandmam before I speak to him. "Well, let me think on this request. If you really want to see those work, I may invite you to one meeting at Bayou St. John. It's possible that someone there will need this medicine, and you may witness the result."

Our discussion goes on for perhaps one hour or longer. Our new acquaintance has many questions. While he listens to the answers, he also makes notes. I can't help but notice that he does have some black hairs sprouting up between his eyebrows. I see nothing on his palms. My saints give me no clear warning about him, but I know I must be cautious with this fellow.

When he moves, he has an almost graceful swaying motion. He stands erect and holds his head high. His teeth, I notice, have sharpness beyond what I am used to seeing. It's true also that I always feel some uneasiness when I'm near him. I think now to ask him about his life in France, as he prepares to leave.

He reaches for his cape that hangs on a rack near the front door, wrapping it around his shoulders, then he turns to bid us a goodnight.

"Ah, Monsieur, I wanted to ask you about your home in France before you go."

He looks surprised at this request. "What would you like to know, Mademoiselle Lalin?"

"I've never been to the country. I picture castles with gardens and fountains on the grounds. Is your home like that? Your calling card describes a dukedom."

He blinks and puckers up his lips. "Sad to say, that my castle was destroyed by fire some years ago. Only three walls remain. A turret rises at the end of one wall. The castle moat has fallen into ruin. Unfortunately, no one in my family has the means to restore."

"And how was it called?" I ask.

"*Le Mistral*, like the wind. Have you heard of it?" He adjusts his black top hat and moves toward the door. "I bid you a good evening. I'm afraid I must be on my way. Another appointment awaits me before I am done this day." He smiles, as he makes his slight bow. "We'll meet again." And he is out through the door before I have time for more questions.

Grandmam and I stand in silence for some few minutes while we hear the gate slam shut. There're no carriage sounds, however, so I listen for his footsteps along the banquette.

One quick decision I make. I turn to Grandmam, rub my palms together, pressing prayer hands to my lips. I take a deep breath before revealing my plan. "It's time for me to shift to my feline form. This tuxedo cat needs to learn more of Dr. Lycus and his connections in the city."

Chapter Eighteen

It only takes me minutes to shapeshift. Grandmam opens the gate and I scoot out onto the banquette. Of course, I expect to see the Dr. Lycus striding down the next block or turning at the corner, but he's not in sight.

I run full speed in the exact direction of his last footfall. At the first corner, looking both ways, I see only two old women trading stories on a doorstep. Racing on along Rue St. Anne, I reach the next corner, where a drunk man has fallen at the curb and a sailor bends to help him up. It's dark along these roads, but with my cat eyes I can see most clearly. It's late. There's no one else out on that block.

At the next corner, a fair-skinned cocotte calls down from her window. She's talking to two men who stroll together on the opposite corner. I see them look up just when she bends forward so her lowcut blouse shows off her ample cleavage. These fellows smile but keep on walking down the banquette.

I continue padding my way along, but it seems I've lost the trail of my visitor. He left no scent for me to follow. So it is that I decide to wander through the Quarter a bit before returning home.

It must be near midnight. Gambling houses and saloons are open.+ Still not too many folks outside. Loud voices travel through a few open doors and windows. When I turn one corner onto Rue Royal, I see a carriage slowing down in the middle of the block. It stops completely at the door of one grand old mansion. A gate stands beside the house. I creep closer, dodging in and out of doorways. With my black coat, it's easy to conceal myself at night.

I'm very close now. The gate's a wide one with cherubs sculpted on the top of the wrought iron entrance way. I wait and listen near the vehicle. It's not an open carriage, so the driver speaks to the passengers inside.

"We're at the address, Monsieur," he calls out.

The carriage door swings open. I see a top hat and for a moment I think that I have caught up with Lycus Volcain after all. When the man steps out, I stare in the darkness and try to determine if this is the Abel who Etienne and I have spied on at the cabin in the woods near to Bayou St. John.

Yes, it is him, Abel, the loup garou, who attacked us on the Isle Deniere last year. While I stand there in the darkness in my furry feline form, I recall all the turmoil of those awful times. We stayed for a short time on that strange isle, hiding from the city police. Etienne had been accused in his wife's death by poison. We were saved when proof of his innocence became clear to the police. The true villains were finally discovered and with that we regained our normal lives again.

But now I watch as Abel pauses on the curb and pays the driver. Then I have a real surprise. He speaks to someone still inside the carriage. A woman slides out and he lifts her down to the walkway with some effort I would guess, as she's a bit overweight herself.

Mon Dieu, I say inside my feline head. The Yvette is with him too. She wears a full silk gown. It looks to be a shade of lavender. What a lovely dress with small silk roses sewn along the bodice and extra pleats to conceal her plump waistline. A shawl, she's draped around her shoulders. Her dark hair's covered with a scarf, but a few ringlets spring out around her ears. A breeze blows them against her cheeks, and she reaches to tuck the wispy curls back behind the cloth. She stands beside Abel. I creep in closer, so to hear what might be said.

A bit of luck I have. They knock now at the tall oak door by the iron gate. Nothing happens. No one comes. Yvette nudges him, and he knocks again. Still the door doesn't open.

"Don't you have a key?" she asks, pointing to his pocket.

"I'm not sure," he says, checking both his coat pockets. He pulls out a set of keys, sorts through them and picks one out. It doesn't fit the keyhole. He goes through the set now. None of them fit the lock.

She stomps her foot and sighs so loudly that it's almost like a groan. "What shall we do?"

Abel grasps the back of his own neck. "*Sacrebleu*," he mutters like a curse and stuffs all the keys back into his pocket.

But then comes the biggest surprise of all. Yvette pulls her shawl off her shoulders, and slings it at her friend, Abel. She shakes her head, reaches into to the small drawstring bag she carries and pulls out a small bottle. Leaving Abel to stand there at the door, she moves toward a narrow alleyway, but stops once to glare back at him.

She disappears into the darkness and I dare not follow. I would certainly be noticed by one of them at this point.

Abel bites his lower lip, knocks once more at the door before he takes a slumping walk towards the blackness of the alleyway. He looks both ways up and down Rue Royal, and then joins his lady friend in the darkness. Although they have disappeared around that corner, I feel a tension that makes my fur stand on end.

Five minutes pass. What fans the air inside that alley? I hear some rustling sounds. A whoosh, a brush against the walls on each side. Then a deep throated growl breaks through the other noise.

I creep outside the doorway where I've been hiding, but now I freeze there on the banquette and scramble back against the building wall.

What a frightful sight! Giant wings emerge first. A huge bat I think it is or something like that. Lifting in the night air, the wings stretch toward the night sky, higher than the doorways. The creature struts and flutters forward. Right behind it comes the snapping jaws of loup garou. I pray they do not spy me backed tight against the wall. I lie low and duck my head to hide my white spots. The growling monster leaps in the air with grinding teeth, and I think that I am dead for sure this time.

The winged creature squawks. It whips one wing at the loup garou. He turns and yelps an angry cry, but then leaps onto its back. With flapping wings this thing lifts itself with the hairy monster clinging to it.

I feel the air rushing all around me, as the two together rise above Rue Royal and slowly higher, higher to near the building's upper floors. My small body quivers, while I watch. Ah, she must intend to make a landing on the top story of this house. If that's the case, I guess they will find a way to enter on the roof. There's no longer any way for me to see them, especially with my short feline legs.

My furry tail turns bushy. I crouch low along the banquette and breath deep to bring back my calmer self. While I wait for some minutes, I listen for the sounds this pair will make. Scrambling noises float down to me. Something bangs against a window or a door and then there's a long silence.

I'm not sure how much time has passed, but when I look up again, there's a lamp burning now in a room upstairs. Thoughts jumble in my head. Whose house is this? Are our enemies living so close to us?

Only half an hour ago I rushed out to follow Monsieur Lycus Volcain, and I end up with this strange encounter with Abel and the plump Yvette. Such an odd coincidence. How I wish I had my Etienne to consult with. But he would tell me to be safe and head for home. Although that could be good advice, I can't help wishing that I could spy on these two shifters.

It's true I now know for sure that Yvette can shift into a flying creature. My intuition always hinted at her shifting powers, but this scene can leave no doubt. I learned that much. Now I look up again and see that two more lamps are shining in the rooms above. If there was only some way for me to climb up and peer inside a window.

I decide to creep over to the carriage gate to see if I can squeeze through the iron bars. Yes, there's space for me. It's a little tight, but my small furry body wiggles in. The gate leads into the courtyard, which is small and has only one small palm tree in the center. It's not likely I can see too much from there, but I dig my claws in and climb to the top. The fronds are floppy, so I hang on to the trunk. Several windows face into the courtyard, but the light is dim. Plus, tonight the sky's blanketed in clouds. No moon gives off a glow to brighten up the darkness.

Then a light goes on near one window. What a stroke of luck this is. Someone inside opens the window, and voices float down to my pointed ears. First, I hear Abel's voice. I catch a few words.

"He should be here by now." But then the sound moves away from the window and only jumbled words travel down to me.

A candle flickers and a figure stands near the opening. It's Yvette. I pray she stands there for a while.

Her voice has a clear, high pitched cadence. "He's on a mission, as you know. He's your master not mine. Sometimes I doubt he'll bring all the help you say he promised." There's a pause. "The air is cold tonight. All windows must be closed."

I hear the shutters slam shut and know that I will hear no more this evening.

Chapter Nineteen

I wake this morning in my own bed after one long night. Once the window closed off the courtyard at Rue Royal last night, I remained for a short time in the palm tree. Tiredness crept up on me. Only one lamp or candle stayed bright in the upstairs rooms. Time for me to travel home.

I need to send a message to Etienne. It's surprising to find the loup garou stay in a house so near to us. Could this place belong to Madame Nanette? Who were they waiting for? I think it must be Abel's partner, Francois. What connection does Yvette have to Abel? So many questions I ask myself.

Then there's the mystery of Lycus Volcain. How did he manage to disappear just minutes after he had left Grandmam's house? I mull over all these questions while I brew a pot of café in my kitchen room. With a buttered roll, my beverage, and a piece of writing paper I head out to my own courtyard to write a message to my Etienne. After I writing everything, I think he should know, I decide that my best chance to get the message to him will be to take the letter to the docks and find a sailor friend that I know will get it to him.

* * *

More than a week passes, and I hear nothing from my love. I know that he would send a message if his business up the river was still unfinished. My worry grows as each day ends with no word from him.

This morning I wake early with plans to visit Etienne's papa at his office near the docks. I wear my best silk dress and comb my long hair up into a tight chignon. One scarf, I have, matches well with this light blue dress. My cheval mirror guides me, as I take care to wrap the cloth around my hair. Then I find a white straw hat with wide blue ribbon sewn along the brim. At last I feel that I look well enough to see Monsieur Legendre.

The mornings are still cool with this early spring. I look again in my armoire and choose a soft, light cloak to complete my look. Worry for my protector occupies my mind. I don't know his papa so well, although I'm sure he likes me, as he was with my Etienne at the Quadroon Ball when I became his *placée* choice. I'm my love's mistress that he's contracted to care for and with his papa's approval. But my role's to always be at home for his convenience. I have rarely been to the shipping office. As things stand with Etienne's disappearance, there's no doubt I must go to learn if his papa knows what's happened.

The walk is not a long one. Merchants wash the banquette in front of their shops as I look down Rue Royal. Creole gentlemen pass me on their way to offices along the river. Some dressed in expertly tailored waistcoats. A few workers from the docks hurry along the side streets. These men wear caps and cotton shirts and loosely fitting vests. One carriage rumbles by as I wait to cross the road. The sun, peeping over roofs, spreads white light across the tiles and shingles on this early morning.

At last I reach the Rue de la Levée where Monsieur Legendre has his office. The front door is open. Several men wait in the foyer of the main office. These men nod at me. I'm glad to see them smile, but I do notice that their eyes narrow just a bit. Of course, they wonder why a young octoroon woman strolls into this shipping office. While there are businesswomen of color in the city, there are none as young as me.

A moment later I see Monsieur Legendre walk out to greet the waiting gentlemen. Now he sees me, and his eyes go wide. He speaks a few words to these customers or associates, but then walks straight up to me, takes me gently by the arm and leads me into another small office.

"Lalin, I'm glad to see that you are well. Etienne received a message that you were ill or injured."

"What?" I step backwards. My voice catches in my throat. "I don't understand."

He closes the door behind us, rubs his chin and stares at me for several seconds. "You have no problems and your grandmama is well too?" He brings his knuckles to his lips and taps them lightly. "Something's not right here, Lalin."

My heart takes a jump. It's like my saints are whispering in my ears, but I can't quite hear what they say.

Etienne's papa sighs deeply before he speaks again. "He returned to the city last night. He had a message that you had great troubles of some sort. I didn't see the note, so I have no details. He stopped by the house for a few minutes and said he had to go to help you. My impression was that you were injured at one of your bayou meetings. But you never heard from Etienne last night?"

"Oh, no, Monsieur, I've heard nothing from him." Tears well-up in my eyes. "Something evil happens here," I say, choking on my own breath.

Coughing, coughing, I struggle to speak again.

Monsieur Legendre leads me to a chair. I slump forward as I sit. Inside my head I tell myself to take control. There's nothing can be done, if I let these fears take power over me. Breathe. breathe deep, I say to myself, and my strength begins to flow again. Quick prayers to my saints I make.

When I look up, Monsieur holds out a glass of water. "Yes, I too feel much concern," he says, as he hands me the glass. "I have my secretary contacting Chief LeBlanc. "Sometimes a friend might play a prank on him, but this seems too serious."

His papa leans back against the desk. He wipes his forehead with one hand. The way the corners of his lips are twisted strikes me as a clearest sign of his distress. I know I must get home or to my grandmam's house to make prayers to St. Michael and the Blessed Mother. My best help always comes from them. Police Chief LeBlanc and his officers never provide the assistance that we need. They only stir up more trouble.

With my self-control returning, I speak to my love's papa in a calmer voice. "Monsieur Legendre, please keep me informed of any news you learn, and I will do the same. I must go now to pray and seek the answers from our holy saints.

He nods. "I know you have a strong faith to guide you. I will check with our friends and family to see if there's been any contact. We'll call a carriage ride for you now. Take care and pray for all of us, *mon cher*."

✱ ✱ ✱

I have the carriage driver drop me at Grandmam Selene's. She offers comfort to me, and I value her opinions and solutions. Through the gate I go, telling myself that I will not burst into tears. Panic has no value. I must keep my head clear to find my love.

Grandmam greets me at her door, and I tell her what Monsieur Legendre described to me. "I've prayed for calmness, and the saints have blessed me with a clear head."

"Prayers, yes, prayers and offerings must be made. I'll get the candles ready, Lalin. You may find some rum and fruits for offerings in my kitchen room. Bring the finest liqueurs. Sometimes it's best to include the most expensive gifts."

We prepare a beautiful candle circle. I carve his name on one tall white candle and place it in the center. The offerings we spread behind the candle.

Grandmam brings out a small vessel with sea salt that's been blessed by the priest.

"Take a pinch, Lalin, and place it over the door frame. You may stand on that stool." She points to the piece. "After that you'll take another pinch and put it under the doormat."

These directions I follow. She whispers some words to me. I kneel and begin to sing a chant.

> *Our holy mother, who we call Erzulie.*
> *We place the ocean salt on our door to draw my Etienne*
> *from the heavens to the ever-flowing seas.*
> *Ships sail all seven seas so let me call the powers of these waters*
> *to send an image of my love.*

I rise now and light the tall white candle. We let it burn in the center for ten minutes, while I visualize my Etienne. In my mind I see him. He stands in front of me for an instant. I embrace his image. Erzulie takes me in her control, and I begin to spin around the room. I feel her in my body breathing her sweet breath. And now I fall to the floor. The vision comes to me.

A mist rises, and I see him in its center. *Bon Dieu,* a fine room he lies in, but he's stretched out on a bed. He moves, but his eyes are closed. What's happening here?

There's a sound. Someone's knocking at the door. Etienne sits up slowly like some sleeping potion hinders him. He says, "Who's there?"

"It's me, *mon amour.*" A woman's voice.

What's this house? Something seems familiar. I can see confusion on his face. The door swings open, and my worst fears come into full view. She wears a lacy dressing gown, a violet shade that compliments her fair complexion. The plump Yvette waltzes in to stand beside his bed.

He shakes his head. "How did I get here? I must be dreaming!"

"Ah, you are one of us now. I've been searching for you for a year."

Chapter Twenty

"Lalin, Lalin." Grandmam Selene holds my shoulders. I feel my body shaking. "You screamed in your trance," she says. "I felt I had to wake you." She sighs, "I shouldn't have disturbed you, but your face showed me pain. I couldn't help myself."

I groan, pull myself up from my place inside the candle circle. The white candle with Etienne's name carved on it lies on the floor. It's cracked now in the middle. My chest feels tight. A heaviness grows in my body. No words come to me. I struggle to take some deep breaths. Grandmam is pouring something into a glass. This liquid she hands to me, and I realize that she gives me rum from the offerings of the altar.

For some few seconds I stare at the glass, and then I gulp it down in several swallows. Coughing, coughing, I think that I might spit up this fine rum drink, but I manage to keep it down. My throat's burning with the heat, but I know it's like a strong herb to bring me calm once again.

"My worst fears. I had a nightmare. He's been taken by Yvette and her loup garou. I need to call the trance back. If he's where I think, then he's in a house right here in the Quarter."

Grandmam takes the glass from me and fills it up again. "You must take some time to think this through, Lalin." All these things happening this morning brought too much stress. When I saw that pain on your face, I grabbed you by the shoulders. I've never seen you look like that. It frightened me."

I rise slowly, first to my knees and then I stand tall beside my grandmam. "It's what I thought all this time," I say. "I told Etienne that she was after him. Whether it's her wish to have him for herself I can't be sure, but if she despises him for leaving her, then it could mean that she wants to destroy him."

"You rest now, while I pray to our saints. Let me see what I can find out about these monsters."

I know she wants to help me, but I must learn for myself. Grandmam has a stubborn streak, so she'll go ahead even if I object, so I say nothing.

She begins her whispered prayers, lighting more candles as she crawls about on her knees. Her eyes are closed. Her long gray hair flows freely around her shoulders. She starts to tremble first in her hands, but then the shaking moves up her arms and to her torso. All her body quivers. She falls flat inside the candle circle. Several candles topple over, and I am glad I'm there to pick them up, so we'll have no fire here in her house.

A low moan, she makes, jiggling even to her toes. Ah, the words start to filter in between the groans. I can't make them out. It sounds like another language. Maybe one of the old ones from years before she came to our city. While she shudders in her trance, I try to visualize my Etienne again. Yes, I have a clear picture with that look of shock on his face, when he sees Yvette come through the door.

Her image dances in my mind. I never thought she was that pretty, but it seems she's made herself look better. My body tenses. Stay calm I tell myself.

Grandmam begins to mumble louder. With one swift move she turns onto her back. I think for a moment she's getting up off the floor, but then she falls back again, rolling side to side. I watch while she comes to a stillness, opening her eyes.

"Grandmam, you were talking through your trance, but I couldn't understand the words."

She pushes herself up, sitting in the middle of the circle. "The saints gave me a vision of the legend of the loup garou. The stories aren't always the same. I've heard them many times and even seen the results once or twice."

"Did you see Etienne in the dream? It's him that I must know about."

"Yes, I understand the reason for your prayer circle. It looked like him, but I only had a quick view of his face. What I saw was one loup garou attack a man. A fight began. The two wrestled. The creature clawed at the man; blood dripped from his wounds. The victim drew a knife and slashed the wolf man. Then his shape shifted. He changed back into a man. The two rose and stepped apart from the fight. But their blood had mixed. The curse came into being."

"So how do you interpret this apparition? Are the saints giving warnings? What's the meaning?"

She stares at me for one long minute. "It's not for me to say for sure. Those human faces were blank with no features as the vision ended, so I can't tell for certain that it was Etienne. Do you remember the legends of how this curse can work, Lalin?"

"I know that there's more than one belief, and perhaps more than one way to get the curse." I feel tears welling in my eyes again. My fears for my protector grow by the moment.

"The legend in this dream seems clear, but as you say there are several versions. This victim cried that he was unholy. The evil remains with him for one hundred days and one more. After that, the curse could be lifted, and he might live a normal life again."

It's too late for me to stop the tears from coming. I wipe them off my cheeks with the hem of my skirt. Swearing to myself that I will not give into all the ill omens, I thank Grandmam for her help, but it's time for me to go home, make offerings and prayers for myself and Etienne. I must trust that St. Michael and my Erzulie will give me answers that I need. I can't lose faith.

Chapter Twenty-One

When I get to my house on Rue Burgundy, I find a note pushed through the outside louvers of the door. I don't recognize this handwriting. Moving quickly through my foyer into my small parlor, I sit down to read this missive.

My dear Mademoiselle Lalin,
I thank you once again for assisting me with my current research. Your knowledge of the herbal medicine is quite impressive. Could I request another meeting? I know your time is valuable, and I can offer payment for your service. Please advise me of your willingness to meet. If you leave a message with Father Jules at the cathedral, I would be much obliged.
Respectfully yours,
Dr. Lycus Volcain

I have no time to think of this today, but I do place it in a drawer with other notes and messages that I have received. It does occur to me that he speaks of our parish priest as his connection. Strange indeed. I can't picture Dr. Lycus in church.

I walk to the French doors that open on the courtyard. In the corner of my small flowerbed a jonquil blooms. Its sunny shade of yellow brings me a spark of hope that I've not felt this day. But my only thought is to set up my altar for St. Michael, our Legba, and the sweet Blessed Mary. I always have the candles ready on one tea table. A statue of Our Lady rests there too.

I light several candles and bring out my best statue of St. Michael. He wears a tunic, holds his shield in one hand and a sword pointing at the demon with the other. Offerings of wine and cakes I place on a tray.

This prayer session couldn't be more important. I ask for answers. How can I rescue my Etienne? On my knees I plead with my saints to intercede with our *Bon Dieu*. Please fill me with the serenity I need to keep my head clear. Anger fills me. I stare at my statue of St. Michael with his sword. His face shines with the calmness, faith, and goodness that we need to overcome this evil curse.

My parlor begins to fade around me. The familiar mist rises from the floors, as the vision appears. My gift to Etienne, the gold cross, dangles from a desk drawer. An empty room grows around it. My heartbeat sounds in my ears. Deep breaths make me stronger. Where is my love? His emblem hangs, suspended. I need to see my love. Words echo in this empty room.

My prayers are answered. He stands before me now. But he's not alone. A man walks up behind him. Abel. Their lips move, and yet I hear only murmurs.

"Please," I beg my spirits, "let me hear."

Then one word comes through to me, *advantage*. This loup garou man explains to Etienne all the good things he'll earn from his shapeshifting curse.

Etienne moves his lips. His words I can't make out. I hear Abel again. He's leaning very close to my protector, and at the same time it's as if I can feel him near to me. Chills wrap around my neck as I feel his breath on me. I'm not sure how this happens, but the saints have made my spirit part of his. I have a strong sense of his consciousness and yet still maintain my own.

"*You'll find there're many benefits. Most of us have success in this world. We take control where we need to, and otherwise we live lives like normal people. I think you will agree.*"

I hear these words from Abel, but no answers come from my Etienne. He closes his eyes and shakes his head. Tiny lines crinkle at the edges of his eyes. Once again, his lips move. He bites his lower lip. His sadness I can feel for myself. I speak to St. Michael and Our Blessed Mary. *Let me see inside his head. Is he thinking now of me? Please let this curse be lifted and tell me what to do next.*

Someone knocks against the door. Abel doesn't turn to see who's there. His voice rises again. "*My cousin feels some passion for you. It's her obsession that's brought you to this state.*" He shrugs. "*Yvette insists that she must have you. Believe me she'll work all the charms she can muster.*"

"No, no." I say out loud. My hands begin to tremble. My breath catches in my throat.

Knuckles, banging louder than before, rattle louvers on my door. My consciousness comes to me slow but steady. The image starts to fade. The sound is at my own front door. Who's there?

✴ ✴ ✴

Candle flames flare, as I focus on the room again. I hear my name called outside my door.

"I'm coming," I call out, rising from the floor. It takes me several minutes to get my mind back to this time and place. I stumble in my haste to find out who this visitor is. I unlock the inside door and flip the latch to open the louvers. No one's there, so I push through to look up and down the banquette.

"Monsieur," I shout, "Doctor Lycus, wait."

His cape flies out in the breeze. He's almost reached the corner of Toulouse but stops short and swings around to face me. "Mademoiselle Lalin, you're home after all."

"I am, Monsieur. How may I help you?"

He hurries back towards me with his swaying walk. "I had a visit with another friend who lives here on Rue Burgundy, and heard your home was only some few blocks away. My apologies for knocking at your door in this unannounced fashion, but I've been so anxious to meet with you again." With a slight bow, he reaches for my hand. His lips feel warm against my fingers. It's strange, but even with all my doubts about him I almost find that I'm glad he's here.

"I did receive your note a short while ago and read your request that I leave a message with Father Jules at the Cathedral. I was surprised that you had that connection."

He smiles and nods. "Yes, yes, the priest and I met years ago in France. We've always kept in touch."

This news makes me take another look at my new acquaintance. Perhaps he is a person I can trust. Still I hesitate to invite him in, and we stand chatting on the banquette at my door. My worries for Etienne swirl in my head, as I listen to Dr. Lycus describe his latest thoughts on herbal remedies.

"Well, Lalin, once again I do apologize for appearing unannounced in such an uncouth manner, but perhaps you will agree to meet with me sometime soon."

In my distracted state, I shrug and nod. "Yes, I'd be pleased to meet you."

"*C'est fantastique*," he says with such enthusiasm that I flash a smile at him. "Perhaps at the market this afternoon or tomorrow, whichever time is best for you." He takes a pocket watch from his vest, glances at it, then puckers up his lips and continues. "I have to see some friends of mine on Rue Royal early in the afternoon, but mostly I am flexible."

Rue Royal brings me back to Etienne since I am sure he's there in that house with Abel and that Yvette. I see it in my head. Cloudy, but clear enough for me to know.

I must have stood in silence for some minutes, before Lycus Volcain tapped me lightly on the arm. "Are you feeling well? A sad look came over you just now."

I come back from the pictures in my head. My thought is that I should go to the Cathedral this afternoon and see Father Jules. He will have some advice for me. With that in mind I tell Lycus Volcain that I plan to meet him at the market at half past noon.

"Look for me among the sellers of the gris-gris and herbal potions," I say. I can also check on Apolline while I'm there. It has been almost two weeks since I met last with her.

He makes another slight bow. "Always a pleasure," he says, as he turns and strides towards the corner.

Chapter Twenty-Two

Another vision brings images like paintings from an artist's gallery. The saints give me a sign that I must speak with Father Jules. It's not quite noon and yet so much has happened this day already. I'm confident that it's most important that I seek his council before my visit to the market.

I freshen up a bit, but still wear my best silk dress with the matching tignon and the white straw hat. The walk's a short one. I know there will be a Mass shortly after noon, so I can catch the priest before he changes to his vestments.

A small garden flourishes at the rear of our church. As I pass, Father Jules is unlocking the back door. He's halfway through the entrance before I reach the garden gate. This priest always gives me sound advice. I feel comfortable with this man in his mid-years, old enough to be my father. He's a Creole man with skin an olive tone. His eyes, deep-set, impress me as does his hawkish nose.

"Father, may I please speak to you for a moment," I call out to him.

He stops so suddenly that he almost stumbles on the threshold of the door but catches his balance and turns to face me. "Ah, Lalin, are you coming in for Mass?"

"I can't stay today, Father Jules, but I'm hoping you can help me with a few questions."

"Of course," he says and motions for me to follow him in. We're at the back of the Sanctuary, as we enter, and he leads me to a quiet spot at the side of the Nave. Some parishioners have arrived. They kneel, praying in the pews. Some few look up to see us.

He whispers, "We should talk in the Narthex, Lalin, so as not to disturb the people in their prayers. There I can greet the faithful as they enter, and you tell me how I can help you." He pauses near the holy water fount and gives me a kind smile.

"I know you don't have much time to consult with me now, Father. But I must ask you what you know of a man called Lycus Volcain. His calling card states that he's a medical doctor coming from France."

My priest looks surprised and hesitates before he speaks. "Hmm, yes, Lycus is an old acquaintance. We were friends in fact when we were young even before I entered the priesthood."

"Then he is a person that's worthy of trust?"

"He does not attend Mass or follow the faith as you and I do. However, we sometimes get together to discuss his medical theories. Has he consulted you about your herbal remedies? I know that he's come here to research the local ways with potions and healing practices."

"Yes, I have had meetings with him. He appears to be honest, but I've had some uneasy feelings about him at times." I want to tell Father about my visions of Etienne, but I know there's no time for that, so I ask another question. "May we speak again, Father? Perhaps this evening after dinner."

"You are troubled aren't you, *mon cher*? Yes, of course, stop by the rectory before dark, and we will have more time to talk."

I thank the priest and agree to meet with him at the later hour.

✳ ✳ ✳

It's nearly one o'clock when I see my friend, Apolline, setting up her table at the market. She recognizes me coming through the stalls and waves.

"How are you, *mon poussin*, my chickadee?" she calls to me. "I have a late start today, because my ride to market came late."

I give her my warmest hug. "So good to see you, Apolline, and you are looking well."

She looks behind herself and scans the nearby shoppers before she whispers. "Yes, yes, I'm most grateful that I have no more evil trailing after me in recent days. My hope is that I am free from them or they are busy haunting others."

While we're chatting, I keep a watch out for Dr. Lycus. Within some few minutes, a tall shadow falls across a shaft of sunlight between the tented stalls. He surprises me as he seems to come from nowhere. I had only just turned to focus on the crowd.

"Mademoiselle Lalin, here you are." He smiles and takes my hand to kiss.

I see that his sudden motion has startled Apolline. "Dr. Lycus," I say, "may I introduce my good friend, Apolline Carriere."

"*Enchant*é, Madame." He takes her hand, but, when she pulls it away, he nods and takes one step back.

I see some worry on my friend's face, but I say nothing about her look. Instead I try to assure her of this man's uprightness. "Dr. Lycus is a physician who comes from France. He has an interest in our herbal remedies and healing ways. In fact, he plans to write a book about his research of the subject."

The tension in her face begins to ease. She holds out her hand to him. This time he gives it a slight shake but doesn't bend to kiss her fingers. She looks at me again before she speaks. "Forgive me for any slight. Recently my life has been troubled by evil strangers, so my cautiousness may be extreme."

Dr. Lycus frowns and taps one finger against his chin. "Well, Madame, I hope the wicked strangers that you describe have not caused any injury to you."

Apolline sighs and looks as if she may break into tears. "They did indeed cause me injury as well as fright, but with some help from my friend, Lalin, I managed to find peace again and continue with a normal life."

Dr. Lycus turns to me now, as if looking for some explanation for this story coming from a woman that he met only moments ago.

My head fills with odd thoughts as we stand there in silence for some minutes. A picture of the monster spider comes to me. All that misery that troubled my friend for days and days passes through my brain in a series of flashing images. Somehow, I feel I must blurt out some story of the curse that fell on Apolline.

"Evil shapeshifters attacked her. Fortunately, with my grandmam's help we reversed the curse they tried to put on her." I don't say the curse was likely intended for me. There's no need to give him more information. He may be sincere, but I don't feel sure of him.

He stands in silence and rubs three fingers against his lips. At last he speaks again. "I see that you've experienced some hard times together." Clearing his throat, he continues. "I have some knowledge of shapeshifters. In France we have them too, so, if such problems arise again, let me offer help. I've experienced..." This sentence remains incomplete, and he blinks his eyes, smiles, and clasps his hands together. "But we can save my stories for another time. Today I am hoping you can offer me some help. Shall we discuss your herbal medicines?"

Apolline gives me a puzzled look. She may be thinking the same as I am. What indeed does this man know of shapeshifters? Why did he change the subject so suddenly? While I am mulling over questions of my own, Dr. Lycus pulls a paper from his pocket. He begins his discussion like that with one finger pointing to the paper.

"I'm well aware that the thorn apple can be quite poisonous." He's staring at the paper as he speaks. "On the other hand, I know that it is sometimes used here in potions. I thought that you might know about its healing assets."

I'm still thinking that he never finished his remarks on shapeshifters. This seems curious. It's true that his request to meet me came first, and he's pursuing his own interests. So, at this point I decide to let the other subject go.

"Yes, I often use the plant leaves to relieve infections. It's also helpful with pain in muscles and inflammations. The doses must be measured carefully. As you say, large amounts are very poisonous. It's been known to kill."

He's taken a pen out of another pocket to make some notes, while I continue to describe the uses of the thorn apple, sometimes called datura. Apolline remains with us, and I can see that she's absorbing the information on her own.

"There's another usage that you may be aware of Dr. Lycus. The thorn apple is known to cause hallucinations in certain doses. These may calm a person with disorders of the mind."

"Ah, tell me more about this usage." His face brightens when he asks me this.

"Much knowledge you need before working with this plant. It can be used to bring out the powers of our saints, but danger can be involved. Visions come and go. There must be strong control of portions."

Dr. Lycus's eyes grow wide, and he takes a long deep breath. "If you could teach me about this plant, I would be grateful. I can even pay you for your time."

I need to think on this request. He must have all the facts to understand how to measure pieces of the leaves and flowers. And even, if he has the time to learn, he's sure to make mistakes if he tries to use it often.

Standing tall, I give one firm answer. "I need time to decide what I can show you of the treatments. Doses that cause the dreams I can't reveal, as this can go against the saints."

"I see," he says, and his eyes narrow. "Well, I will check my schedule, and I hope we'll meet again soon, Lalin." Pulling out his pocket watch, he nods. "Another meeting requires me to leave now. *Merci*, I'll send a missive to you soon."

Chapter Twenty-Three

I return to my house on Rue Burgundy. Apolline and I agree to meet again this week. Still I've told no one except Grandmam Seline about my dreams of Etienne and the loup garou. A tiredness runs through my veins. It's almost dinner time, and I decide to take a rest. Lying back against the cushions on my chaise longue, I doze off.

Dreams fill my sleep. Frightening scenes flow through my mind. I see my Etienne sitting at a table with Abel and Yvette in chairs on either side of him. They're drinking wine with a meal.

Etienne puts his fork down and speaks, "A hundred and one days. It can't be." He shakes his head. "I must make contact with my loved ones..." As he says the words, the image shatters into sparkling flakes like a broken mirror. My body trembles, my eyes open. I'm staring at the ceiling of my parlor.

"By all the saints," I say out loud. "How can this happen?"

* * *

I can't eat. It's like drumbeats in my head, and each stroke brings a pain. The sun sets, spreading shades of pink and gold through clouds that rise above the houses. I make my way to the rectory on a side street near the Cathedral. It's a short walk, and Father Jules opens the door, as if he has been waiting there to hear my knock.

"Come in, Lalin. Tell me; how's your Grandmam Selene? Is she well? And your protector, Etienne?"

My strength slips away. Tears come from the corners of my eyes and roll down my cheeks. The sobs take over. A tremble runs through my body. Weakness in my knees makes me lose my balance, but Father catches me by the arm and leads me into the foyer.

"Sit here," he says and guides me to a bench along the wall. "Geogette," he calls to his housekeeper, "bring a glass of water quick."

I take deep breaths to help me gain back my composure. To weep like this in front of the priest and his servant gives me shame. Footsteps come from the rear of the rectory. Georgette appears with a cup in hand. She's a pretty girl with bright dark eyes. Leaning forward, she smiles at me as she gives me the cup. I thank her.

"*Merci,*" I say. She nods and looks to Father Jules for instruction.

He tells her that I have come in need of counsel. "We'll be in the parlor. Please bring in sherry and perhaps some cakes."

"Let's move to some comfortable seats," he says, takes my arm again and leads me through the archway into a sitting room.

I've never been inside the priest's home before. The room's furnished with a sofa and several chairs. It's comfortable, but perhaps a bit shabby. A large brick fireplace stands out against one wall. A painting of the Blessed Mother, cradling the holy child, hangs above the mantelpiece.

"Relax, *mon cher*, if you wish to speak, I am here to listen."

His kindly voice comforts me. I know I must seek help wherever I can find it. Father Jules knows of the loup garou. But I don't expect that he's had any contact with them. The church is one place that they will most certainly avoid.

How should I begin my story? The priest knows my Etienne and all his family. The Legendres attend Mass every Sunday. In fact, it was Father Jules who performed the marriage of Etienne and his wife, Minette. The poor girl died last year of an evil poisoning. That thought brings a shudder down my spine, but I must speak now.

"Father, my protector, Etienne, has fallen into the hands of the evil loup garou. Believe me, please, he's in the gravest danger. This only happened yesterday. It feels like months ago already. His parents only know that he's disappeared."

And so, I tell my priest of the visions and explain that my Grandmam Selene's the only one that I've shared the facts with, making clear that she too saw the images of Etienne in the house with our enemies. There can be no doubt that he's been kidnapped.

While I continue speaking, Georgette comes in with a tray. A crystal decanter holds the sherry. A dish with several sugar-powdered cala cakes rests at the center of the tray. She nods at us and sets the tray on a side table between our chairs.

Father pours a glass and hands it to me. "The wine will help to calm your nerves," he says.

I take a sip. "I'm looking for any advice you have to give me. My fears overwhelm me. I don't know where to turn."

"But have you actually seen Etienne at this house on Rue Royal? Can you be sure he's there?"

"Our saints show me this, Father. How can they be wrong?"

He leans back against the cushion in his chair and clasps his hands across his chest. "Lalin, you realize that I don't practice with that spirit world that you acknowledge. Even though your faith is strong for the sacraments, your rituals are a mystery to me. I don't criticize. I can only let you know that I see no visions for myself."

I sigh now, wondering if he wants to say that he offers no assistance for me. While I try to think what else I can do, he bends forward towards me and reaches for my hand.

"Lalin, if you give me the address of the house on Rue Royal, I will investigate. I doubt I can gain entrance, but I have other ways of checking. Let me see what I can do. Meanwhile I know that you can shape-shift yourself. If you remember, you let me see that strange gift one time. You could try to gain entrance to the house that way. It might be safest if we make a move together." He takes a sip of sherry for himself then continues. "Tonight, you must get sleep or at least some rest."

"Thank you, Father. My heart pounds so hard I doubt I can sleep."

"Make a sleeping remedy for yourself then. Tomorrow I will meet you at the Cathedral in the morning shortly after sunrise."

Chapter Twenty-Four

Such a long night. A strong potion I make, and still my sleep is restless. Dark dreams come to me. I see Etienne shapeshift, but not into the orange tabby that I love. Instead he grows big ears, red eyes, and sharp fangs. He roams with Abel, the loup garou. His words echo in my ears. "*A hundred and one days with no way to break the spell.*" This dream's a nightmare and not a vision from the saints. My love cannot be transformed by this curse.

Rays of light stream in my windows. I slide out of bed and peer through the drapes. The sunlight hasn't reached the courtyard, but a few bright beams stream across the roof of my kitchen room. No time to waste I say to myself and turn to the armoire against the back wall. A pale blue skirt I choose to wear with a cotton blouse and a gingham tignon to tie around my hair. The café I brew with such speed it's like magic. I sip the brew before I say prayers to the saints and ask for blessings for the day.

It's time to meet my priest. The walk's a short one. Merchants, heading to the market, make up the traffic. Mules and horses pull their carts down Rue Toulouse. Crates filled with fruits and vegetables rattle over cracks along the road as these folks guide the wagons to the marketplace. Two mongrel dogs chase behind the wagons, barking.

When I reach the Cathedral, Father Jules is waiting on the steps. He greets me with a smile.

"We must pray before going to the house, Lalin. There's evil inside and with that there's always danger."

I agree, and we enter through the cathedral's tall doors. At the altar, we kneel. Father Jules takes out his rosary and together we recite the prayers. Inside my head I see our Blessed Mother. With that I know we'll have the saints to intercede with our *Bondye*. We need protection to be safe.

Father recites another blessing before we rise from the altar rail. The sanctity is with us. I grasp my amulet on its chain around my neck. St. Michael's image also brings us safety as we make our way through the sanctuary. The early sunlight gleams through the stained-glass windows, giving glow to all the scenes of our saints, their features brightened by the beams of light.

We are only minutes from the house where Etienne's held captive. Along the banquette we travel, passing a few Creole gentlemen on their way to offices. Most men are still at home having coffee or dressing for the day. They do not work this early. No women walk the street at this hour. At the corner near the house on Rue Royal, we stop. I've pointed out the address, so Father Jules wants to review our plan.

"If I knock, and pretend that I'm looking for an address, it's unlikely they'll invite me in. Also, even in your feline form you would be noticed sneaking in the door."

I sigh and nod agreement. "It's possible for me to slip through the bars of the courtyard gate, but we can't be sure there'll be a window open wide enough for me to slip through on the garden side of the house." I close my eyes for a moment to recall the placement of the windows.

"I'm thinking that I might ask for a map. I could tell them I am lost. If I let them know that I'm looking for a sick parishioner, they could be sympathetic."

I shrug. "I don't sense that they're considerate, kind-hearted people, but who knows how their minds work."

Father rubs his hands together. "Hmm, if you are in your feline form, and you run inside when the door is open, I can say that you're the church cat that followed me from the rectory. In that way I'd push my way in to catch you."

It's truly a funny plan. It sounds so foolish I think it might work to get us inside. And, if we get someone to answer and open the door, it's a sure thing that I could scoot between a person's feet and scamper through the foyer in just a second.

"I think that idea might work. It would cause confusion, being so unexpected, and yet, you'd have the right to catch your own pet."

We stand there at the corner discussing all the possibilities. In the end we both agree to try this way of entry. I tell Father that I will step into a nearby alleyway to change my body shape, and then we'll stroll together to the house which is only a few doors down.

* * *

Hiding in the alley behind some boxes, I pray to my saints to make the change I need. My body shrinks slowly this morning. The stones in the alleyway feel cold against my skin, as I grow small and still smaller. With paws instead of legs and arms, I stretch my back and lick my fur. It's time to pad my way back to meet with Father Jules.

What a look he has on his face when he sees me! I swish my tail and make meow sounds. He smiles and asks if I can still understand what he says to me. When I look into his eyes, he knows the answer. We have our connection, which lets him understand.

Bending to stroke my fur, he says, "Ah, Lalin, you're too amazing. Shall we try our plan?"

I meow and follow as Father walks slowly past several houses. At the fourth house he pauses, it seems he's now uncertain, so I must go ahead and stand squarely in front of the iron courtyard gate in the middle of the block. He follows, standing tall and takes off his hat to smooth back his dark hair.

At the door he knocks, while I hide behind a potted tree. We wait for some few minutes and then he knocks again, this time a little louder. The door swings open and what a surprise I have, as I dare to peep out from behind the tree. The plump Yvette stands in the entrance way. She's well-dressed as always. A deep shade of burgundy she wears. A jeweled comb captures ringlets in a cluster near her neckline.

Father says, "*Bonjour, Mademoiselle.*"

She gives him a tight smile. "May I help you Father?"

The door opens wider. Behind Yvette stands Abel, the loup garou. It's time for me to make my move. I slink slowly from behind the banquette tree. They haven't seen me yet. In a flash I scoot across the walkway and between the feet of all three. Skidding on the hard wood floors, I quickly dodge behind a nearby sofa. Voices follow me shrill and loud. I hear Father exclaiming his apologies, as I see the pairs of shoes circling around the room.

"Close the door, Abel!" Yvette calls out.

While I remain in place, hidden behind the large settee, Father calls out, "*Minou, minou, minou.*" I hear Yvette's anxious voice, mingling with his. Her high heels click against the floor.

I must decide my next move before they pull out the settee and grab a blanket to capture me. I wish I could communicate with my priest. He knows we want to find Etienne. My love's in the house somewhere. When I scrambled in across the floor, I glimpsed a stairway near the center of the room.

Ah, I can hear their footsteps move past the sofa. Yes, yes, it's clear. I know they're not sure where I'm hiding. They look for me down a hallway. I take the chance to creep along behind the furniture. Several large upholstered chairs are lined against the wall. Finally, I reach the stairway. Run now, I say to myself. Etienne may be upstairs.

Scampering at my fastest speed, I fly to the topmost stair. There I pause for some few seconds. Their footsteps clamor up the steps behind me. They must have heard my claws against the wood. I glance behind me to see Abel and Yvette halfway to the top. She lifts her long skirt so high I can see her petticoat. Father Jules stands wide-eyed at the bottom of the steps.

What's my next move? No time to think. A short hall leads to several bedroom doors. Behind me Abel lunges forward almost catching me by the tail. It's then I jump high and out of reach. I skid along the hardwood floors along the hall.

CHAPTER TWENTY-FIVE

I hear a stumbling noise, and then a crash. Abel lunged once again, but this time he trips and slips, falling backwards halfway down the stairs. He cries out. He's hurt his leg somehow. I take this opportunity to scurry down the hallway. All the doors are closed.

On the stairs I hear voices. Yvette is checking Abel's leg, to see if he's badly hurt. Meanwhile I slink along the walls listening for some sound inside the rooms. At the last door in this corridor I can feel his presence. My Etienne's behind this door. I begin to scratch, meow, and rub my body up against the wooden frame.

At first there's no sound, but when I stretch my body up to touch the doorknob with one paw. I hear him. He rises from a chair or perhaps the bed. Footfall comes across the hardwood floor. When the door opens, I jump up against his legs so fast that he yells out in surprise. His eyes are cloudy. Some heavy sleeping potions they're feeding him.

He's unsteadied on his legs, but I think his mind is clear. In an instant he knows me. "*C'est pas vrai*! It's truly my Lalin." He rubs his eyes, bends down, and lifts me up into his arms.

I snuggle against his neck and lick his cheek. We enjoy a brief reunion moment. Heavy footsteps come up behind me. Two hands thrust out, coming from behind my furry head. They grasp Etienne at his shoulders. It's Abel, who grapples with my love. Etienne doesn't have his full strength to pull him off. Strong potions he's been fed. He staggers backwards but manages to catch himself on the bed post. My small body wedges between the two men.

Yvette darts through the bedroom entrance. Her voice is shrill. "It's her. It's Lalin Bonheur. She's a shapeshifter. They've tricked us."

Caught between the two men while they wrestle, I manage to wiggle free. Once on the floor I spin to face Yvette. She assists Abel who struggles to constrain Etienne. They push him back towards the bed again. It seems clear that they've kept him locked in for days here.

More footsteps sound in the hallway, and I see that Father Jules stands at the door. He holds a handkerchief against his head, blotting an ooze of blood on the center of his forehead. When he sees me, he nods, and I give him a loud meow.

It's time for us to make some drastic moves. I dash at Yvette, going under her skirt. Ah, I see her pretty ankle. With one quick pounce, I dig my small sharp teeth into her pale skin. She screams and tries to kick me off, but I cling with all my claw's strength. Now she tumbles backwards, falling hard against the floor. I hear the thud but can't see what exactly happens.

Father Jules should have a chance to make a move. As I crawl out from under Yvette's skirt, the three men are wrestling. Father's strength amazes me. He appears to take control. Yvette hit her head when she fell. She squirms against the floor, rubs her forehead with one hand and then goes limp.

My Etienne thrusts a fist at Abel's chest, but he's weak from the heavy potions. Our priest sees his opportunity and before this loup garou man can catch his full balance, Father slams a hard punch at his chin. I fly in and leap on Abel's leg, digging all my claws through his pants leg into skin. I cling there for moment before he kicks me off his calf. Still his body almost crumbles from the force of Father's punch.

While this is happening, my love has cleared his head enough to reach for a small, bronze statuette sitting on the chest of drawers. He charges forward, catching Abel with the sharp edge of the figurine. It's hard enough to knock him out. He reels for a moment then crashes to the floor.

Father yells to Etienne and me, "Let's go! Run as fast as you can."

Etienne looks at me then whacks Abel one last time with the bronze figurine. The three of us dash through the door and down the stairs with such amazing speed. We're outside the house again, running fast. I'm at their heels as we race down the banquette. Luckily, my protector regains his faculties. He rushes right behind Father Jules. People on the banquette dodge to avoid us. Some stop and stare, as we proceed at top speed.

Father pauses for a moment to look back to see that no one's coming. He knows we've injured them enough to slow them down. "Let's hurry for the Cathedral," he calls out. "If they do come after us, we'll be safe enough in God's house."

And, of course, he's true to his faith as always. These evil shifters find themselves weakened inside the church. Although the stories vary when it comes to limitations of the loup garou, it's certain that their courage fades on holy ground.

We've nearly reached our Cathedral and still we have no pursuers. The daylight's in our favor also. Father Jules leads the way. I feel safe enough as we approach the church to stop. A fast turn into the alleyway, I go to hide my furry self. There I make the change to human form again.

Father and Etienne stand waiting for me at the wide cathedral doors. Once inside the narthex, the entrance room, I dip my fingers in the fount of holy water, cross myself and then turn to my Etienne. His eyes look tired. How pale his skin appears, I'm quick to comfort him.

While I embrace him, his heart pounds hard against my breast. "*Mon amour*, what have those monsters done to you? Some strong herbs they've fed you to make you weak."

"It's true, Lalin. I'm not well. They've tried to ruin me," he whispers.

Our priest opens the sanctuary doors. I take my protector's hand to lead him through and down the aisle, but now I have a big surprise. He jerks his hand away.

He shakes his head hard. "I can't go in, Lalin. Their curse is on me. They say it's set for one hundred and one days or maybe more."

Now I truly gasp with my dismay. "*Bondye!*" I cry out. "This can't be. I thought it only a nightmare. It can't be real."

Father Jules hears my cry and comes back through the doors from the sanctuary. His brow is wrinkled. He grimaces. "What's happened, Etienne?" he asks. It's clear my protector's bewildered. He stumbles back from the opening of the church doors.

"He says those monsters gave him the curse." I close my eyes as I say the words. My breath catches in my throat. It's misery I feel. "Father, what can we do? There must be something."

Father stands in silence for so long that I feel he's powerless to even answer. Then he moves closer to us. "Are you certain of this, Etienne?"

"I've had only one transformation. I don't know how it happens. They say it's in the full moon time, but Abel and his friend have their own controls. They change at will. And, yes, I'm certain that I have this evil in me. It's in my blood."

Our priest shakes his head. My eyes fill with tears, so that all's a blur around me. "There has to be a cure," I say. "Father, please, the faith will give you answers."

Chapter Twenty-Six

Three days have passed since we freed my Etienne from his captivity. We've seen no signs of Abel or Yvette. After one long discussion with our priest, my love decides not to explain this bizarre curse to his family. Father told them that we managed to free him from a ring of thieves who planned to hold him for a ransom. I know our priest is troubled with the lie, but he fears the real story will be much too much for them to accept.

His parents expressed their gratitude to Father Jules, who made it clear that I'd been his assistant in the rescue. My protector's papa sent me huge bouquets of flowers along with many other gifts. Knowing nothing of the evil business that still haunts us, he's grateful to see his son again. So far Etienne hasn't had a transformation. I thank the saints for that and send many prayers and offerings to them. Father says Mass for my love even though he can't attend.

But the evil signs begin to appear. He's sprouting hairs between his eyebrows. Some dark strands grow from his palms. I'm careful to remind him to shave these away. Melancholy takes him over sometimes. He says he feels no difference inside his head but worries all the time that he'll change without warning. He has no inkling of the will to make a change. On the full moon he plans to lock himself away. Meanwhile our priest researches in his library, reading all the scriptures, books, and documents to find a solution. One antidote calls for throwing salt on the body of the loup garou, when it attacks. But this deterrent is not a cure.

In these last few days, I've spent much time with Grandmam Selene. We burn many candles in our prayers. Even at the bayou meetings with my followers, I always make offerings to Erzulie for Etienne. My people dance with me, and St. Michael comes to ride me near the bonfire. Still no answers come.

Visions frighten me. Dreams haunt me through the night. Images of my love transforming. Shifting shape. Fangs grow between his lips. His eyes gleam red as blood. Head and face change slowly. His normal nose becomes a snout. Long black hair grows through his skin. It's then I scream out in my sleep. Etienne shakes me gently in our bed to wake me from this nightmare. When I open my eyes, he's still his handsome self.

His eyes, filled with sadness, look down at me. He rises from the bed and begins to pace across the room. Even though our love remains strong, there's tension in his every movement. He pauses, leans forward to give me kisses, but even as we embrace, I feel the tightness in his body. I feel sensitive to his worries. Evil hangs in the air, invisible but heavy still. It's like a gray cloud draped around him. Even with all the troubles he stands erect. My beautiful man still thrills me with firm muscles, fine skin and such a strong, straight body.

He brushes one strand of hair off his smooth forehead. "Lalin, the full moon will rise within a few days. Soon I have to find a place to hide. I must be locked up before the sun goes down. If you can, help me find a secure place to hide."

I'm not sure what to do about this. My plan is to ask Grandmam Selene. She does much better working ways to handle wickedness. I know she'll have some idea of what to do to protect others from any violence he may cause. But I also fear for him since many carry knives in this city. A silver blade can kill or injure loup garou when he takes this form. Even though it's said that one needs a silver bullet to stop the wolf man, I still believe that any bullet can do harm. I can't bear to think of him in pain.

"Try not to worry so much," I say. "We will find a way to keep you in a safe place. And Father Jules will soon locate the remedy or means to break this evil bond they put on you."

He sighs. "I fear for you, Lalin, and for others. My family doesn't even know what's happened to me. Mama would be terrified. They are concerned that I avoid them. Of course, I see Papa at the office, but I worry when I visit at the house. What's to become of us?" With another sigh, he shrugs his shoulders. Yet he turns to kiss me once more. "I must dress now for work. Pray all you can for me, *mon cher*."

✳ ✳ ✳

Etienne soon leaves for his shipping office. I too dress for the day. While I wrap my tignon around my head, I hear a rattling at my door. A soft knock follows. I think it could be Apolline as we planned to get together so that I may give her more lessons on making herbal remedies.

I unlock my door and lift the latch that secures the outside louvers. Standing tall, his full cape, and a long gray scarf wrapped around him, Dr. Lycus Volcain greets me with the curling smile he always shows.

"*Bonjour*, Lalin," he says, lifting his hat and giving me a formal bow. "I was passing through your neighborhood again and thought I might stop by, if only to greet you for a moment. I see you're dressed to go out, so perhaps we can stroll up Rue Burgundy together. Which way are you going?"

"I'm on my way to my grandmam's house on St. Ann. If you're walking in the same direction, indeed we can stroll together."

"Excellent," he says. "I stopped by one time before, but you weren't at home. I know I said that I would send a message, but it seems I never have the time. So how are you and your protector, Etienne?"

When he mentions Etienne, I feel my lips tremble. Somehow, I can no longer keep my composure whenever someone asks about my love. "We're well." I lie to him.

I know he's much too clever not to notice my facial change, but I have no reason to discuss my personal problems with him. There's still a doubt in mind about his motives. He walks beside me on the banquette, continuing past Toulouse. I feel his eyes search my face. We stroll up Burgundy in silence.

When we reach the next corner, he stops and turns to me. "I believe you have troubles, Lalin. It's hard to see such a lovely girl as you with a sad look and suffering in her eyes. As you know I hold some credentials and knowledge in several fields. Please believe me. I can offer help or support."

"I thank you for your concern, Monsieur. It's true. We have some troubles, but I'm not free to talk about things. The burden is on my Etienne. He's the only one to discuss the problem."

"Hmm, I see." He puckers up his lips and nods. "I hope he'll have his dilemma solved soon in any case. Please tell him of my concern."

We reach the next corner, and Dr. Lycus stops and extends a hand to me. "I turn here. In case you or Etienne decide to confide in me, leave a message with Father Jules." He gives my hand a squeeze. "Many problems I've solved in my time. My patients have sometimes been amazed by the vastness of my skills." He tips his hat again and gives me his mystic smile. With one quick turn he proceeds along the cross street.

* * *

Grandmam brews café in her kitchen room when I arrive. I walk through her courtyard and call out to her. She greets me with a warm hug.

"I've finished with my morning prayers," she says. "Let's have our coffee at my dining table. I have some fresh cakes in the house."

She picks up the coffee pot. We walk together across the courtyard. My mind's cluttered with the questions I want to ask, and at the same time, Dr. Lycus's words are ringing in my head. Could it be that he could help us with this curse? Somehow, I always sense he does have some secret knowledge. My memory of the time I tried to follow him comes back to me. He seemed to vanish. Indeed, there's a mystery about him. Even Father Jules implied uncertainty about his past.

In her house, Grandmam tells me she's been praying to the saints about my Etienne. Still she smiles at me, and I know she wants to cheer me. It's time for me to ask her what she thinks we should plan for him as the full moon's phase is almost here.

We set out some cups, saucers, and a plate of cala cakes. She goes out again to get the boiled milk to blend with the coffee. At last we sit and sip from her china cups.

"The saints bring me some answers," she says. "We must find wolfsbane. I believe I can get the leaves we need. There's more to learn. Offerings I can get to make a prayer circle to please the spirits."

"What did you learn of wolfsbane? It offers a fearful poison. It's quite a danger."

"It is, and there are many stories of its use to kill. To murder. But Father Jules has sent a message. He found some information that may lead us to a cure for Etienne's dilemma. He also has some thoughts on where your protector can stay during the full moon phase. He says it might be necessary to have double locks on the room. And make sure too, you have your amulet or a cross with you at all times."

Chapter Twenty-Seven

We set the hour for the meeting with our priest. Grandmam plans to come with me to the Cathedral. With his affliction, Etienne can't enter the sanctuary. Still Father suggests that he come to meet him tomorrow before the final waxing of the moon. There's a carriage house behind the Presbytere, the rectory, with a room attached. Father Jules says the door has a double bolt. He'll use padlocks to secure. The two windows have bars. Inside there'll be a cot but no other furniture.

In the evening, the two of us arrive at the Presbytere to see the room. Through the house we go and out the back door. The room is along the side of the carriage house. I check the windows, as Etienne has instructed me to do. Iron bars stretch across the glass. The walls are made of brick. We examine the double bolt on the door. It all looks quite secure.

Food and water will be left by the cot. Father believes that the door is strong and can't be broken. Even if a loup garou breaks out the window glass, he won't be powerful enough to bend the bars. There's no fireplace with a chimney, which might offer an escape route.

Although, as a wolfman, my protector may try to rip down the walls with his supernatural powers, we believe he can't escape. Grandmam Selene and I plan to make a strong sleeping potion to feed him over two or three days before the final phase. If these herbs calm him, his transformation might be easier.

Before we leave the priest's house, we thank Father for providing this safe confinement for Etienne. I ask him what he's learned of cures for this evil thing. He has been searched for days, he says, and tells us something of his finds.

"There are several plants listed in the arcane manuscripts I found in the Cathedral library. Ancient remedies in a catalogue printed at least a hundred years ago. These are mixed in with the rituals described for exorcisms and ..."

Grandmam interrupts, "Beg pardon, Father, but I must ask if the wolfsbane's mentioned?"

His eyes go wide. "Yes, yes! And it's called monkshood in the manuscripts. I need time to study these pages. There's mention of a sample of the loup garou's blood would be needed to break the curse."

"Father, I can't thank you enough for all you've helped us with. I'm wondering could Grandmam and I see these pages you've found?"

"Let me find a time to meet you at the library. Yes, you can read about the exorcisms and the wolfsbane cures. I pray we'll come to some conclusion for a remedy."

* * *

The full moon will rise this evening. Etienne has left his office for the day. We sit together in my parlor this afternoon too tense to even share our passion. I pour two glasses of red wine. We sip in silence for some time.

"We will resolve this, *mon amour*," I say to him. "I know tonight's a fearful time or us and most especially you."

Pressing both hands against his temples, he bends forward, clears his throat then turns to me. "I feel a pressure in my chest," he says, breaths deeply and continues, "whatever happens this night isn't even the worst fear. At least I know I'll be secured."

"But Father Jules has found a treatise with the remedies for the malady. There is a cure for..."

Etienne interrupts me. "I didn't tell you-- I did see Abel yesterday near my office. He tipped his hat to me like we were old friends. I was so unnerved that I ran back into the building. When I came in breathless, my father saw me and asked what the matter was."

My heart jumps nearly to my throat. "But why didn't you tell me?" Just the mention of this monster makes me shiver. He will use all his powers to control my love. My worst fears shift through my mind.

"I didn't want you to be as upset as I was."

"Do you think they may be planning something? We should be very watchful until we get you to the Presbytere." I grasp my amulet and look to see if Etienne wears his gold cross. "*Mon Dieu*, where's your cross? I gave it to you after the rescue on Rue Royal."

Etienne frowns. "I can't wear it now, Lalin. It burns my skin."

I move closer to him and pull his shirt open at the neck. Indeed, I see the tiny blisters on his skin. "And you said nothing, Etienne." An anger fills my head, and I stand up. Is there no way I can protect my love? Now holy medals burn his skin. "We have more danger than I thought."

"Lalin, I tried to put it on more than once. I didn't want you to have another worry. *Mon Coeur*, we haven't far to travel to the priest's house, and my carriage's waiting at the corner of Toulouse.

With a groan, I turn from him and pace across the floor. "Grandmam will be coming soon. We have to get her to contact Father Jules and have him come here. I fear trouble getting to the Presbytere. If Father's with us, we'll have a better chance."

Etienne nods, but says nothing. He closes his eyes, and I realize how tired and tense he must be. I go to him again. Kneel in front of him and take his hands in mine.

"Please know that I'll do anything to save you from this evil." I rise and sit beside him. One long kiss we share. Our arms tangle in an embrace. With tight muscles we linger there for some minutes.

I hear Grandmam Selene's voice at my door, so quickly I go to let her in. Her eyes show the fearfulness. I tell her about how Etienne saw Abel only yesterday. "And he can't wear his cross. Now it burns his skin. He has blisters on his chest."

Her lips twist into a scowl. "It's worrisome indeed," she says.

"Could you go quick to get Father Jules and bring him here? It's our best chance to make sure we can get Etienne to the secured room."

Grandmam agrees, and she's off without a hesitation. "But do be watchful as you go," I call out to her as she hurries along the banquette and turns the corner at Toulouse.

Less than an hour later she's at my door again. This time our priest is with her. I let them in, while Etienne sits hunched over on my sofa.

"Father's given us four more crosses to carry." Grandmam holds two large carved wooden amulets and two gold ones. "We can put one cross at Etienne's feet to give him some protection," she says.

I lead them into my parlor where they both greet Etienne and add good wishes to cheer him.

"We'll use my carriage," Father says. "I don't think they would recognize it. Do you have a saber from your fencing practice or a pistol?"

Etienne pats his vest pocket. "A pistol, yes, I've been carrying one since my escape."

"*C'est bon*. We should have at least one hour before the sun sets. It's the best time for us to leave and get you secured for the night." Father Jules makes sure that Etienne carries extra clothing.

Grandmam helps me wrap my tignon around my hair securely, and the four of us leave my house. Father's carriage is parked outside my door. He leads his horse to a water trough before we climb in. Then Etienne helps Grandmam up to her seat, and I climb in on the other side. No time to waste.

It's not a long ride to the priest's house, but there're many wagons traveling through the Quarter this time of day, which slows us down. We decide to steer the horse down Burgundy and take Rue St. Ann across to get there.

The wagons clear out as we approach St. Ann. This route is quieter. Father urges his horse to trot a bit faster after we turn the corner. I sigh out loud in relief that we're almost at the priest's house. Surprisingly, no one's walking on the banquette, and our carriage is the only one on the street. I bend over to see if the wooden cross has slipped behind the seat. It's still there and push it forward so it's near our feet.

One more block to travel and we'll reach our destination. My gold cross lies on my lap. I make sure to keep my fingers touching it. Etienne sits beside Father Jules. Another cross lies close to our priest. It's then I hear some strange noises coming from above us.

When I look up, I see it. Grandmam's staring up like me, and we both yell out at the same time. "Watch out!"

Enormous wings flutter above Rue St. Ann. A bird, larger than an eagle or even a great heron, crisscrosses through the air above us. First it circles then comes a dive down towards the carriage. Its long sharp beak comes straight towards my Etienne. Grandmam swings her wooden cross above our heads. The creature soars up, but then dives again. On this second plunge it opens its beak, makes a cawing sound, and tries to clamp onto Etienne's waistcoat collar. What amazing strength it has! His collar's in the creature's beak. Father reins back the horse, just as my love is lifted off his seat.

CHAPTER TWENTY-EIGHT

Screaming, I reach to grab the bird by its wings. Its black eyes singe my skin. Feathers drift around me. I lose my grip.

With Etienne's collar in its beak, the creature grasps his shoulders with its talons. My love twists his body to shake it loose. Its claws still cling to him. He strikes hard with his fists and struggles to pull the talons from his shoulders. Now he reaches for the pistol in his pocket. The monster drops off his shoulder to sink its claws into his arm.

Father swings his whip and a cascade of feathers flies in all directions. Grandmam thinks clearly enough to lift a large cross and thrust it towards the head. A screech vibrates in my ears and echoes off the nearby buildings. When the gold cross touches it between the eyes, I see more feathers burst off its head. Smoke fills the air. Grandmam hits it with the amulet once more. Its talons lose their grip. It squawks again.

There's no one on the street to call for help. Even at the corner no carriages are coming down our way.

Etienne draws his pistol. The bird sails back and soars up with a piece of collar cloth still clinging to its claw. My protector fires his weapon. Further up the creature goes. But when he fires a second time, the bird screams, and wobbles in the air. Still it continues to climb, flapping wings towards the rooftops. It turns, fluttering wildly. Agitation clearly visible even at this distance. Dark blue feathers swirl above us in the breeze. I think it readies for another dive. But instead it rises above the nearby roofs, flaps above the chimneys, and disappears as suddenly as it came.

"Is anyone hurt? I hope the creature took a bullet! *Mon Dieu*! What a monster! " Father looks bewildered, as he steers the horses forward once again.

Etienne checks his pistol, places it on the seat beside him and turns to me. "No one's hurt, but most unnerved for certain. I've only a few scratches from the talons," he says and shakes his head. "I'm sorry that these enemies attack your carriage, Father."

"What enemy? What was that thing?" Father asks. "Do you know?"

Etienne clears his throat. "The story gets complicated. It could be the woman, Yvette. If she's a shifter, it's almost certain. They want to control me. Ruin my life if they can."

I hold my tongue. But it's clear to me that she's wanted my Etienne for herself. If she can't have him, perhaps she hopes to destroy him.

We reach the carriage gate of the Presbytere. Father climbs down to unlock the entrance. Everyone stays quiet, looking dazed. I feel the tension in every nerve and muscle. At last we're in the courtyard, and our priest helps Grandmam down from her seat.

The courtyard's filled with shadows as the sun has reached its low point in the sky. Etienne and I climb out, and I collapse into his embrace. He holds me close for some few seconds. Tears trickle from the corners of my eyes. If these monsters want my powers, why do they aim their punishments on Etienne? But then I do know what Yvette wants, and determines to have her way at any cost. At least the cross burned her. She might have a bullet in her wing.

Father Jules leads us into his house and calls his servant girl, Geogette, to bring out some wine. "We need to calm our nerves," he says.

While we sit for some few minutes, I keep a watch through the windows to see the sun's near to setting. The full moon rises soon.

* * *

Etienne prepares himself for cloistering. Grandmam and I kneel with him in the room next to the carriage house. Father gives his blessings. We burn incense. I stay behind with him when our priest and my grandmam say their last prayers and wish him a safe passage through the night.

"We will get through this, my love," I say to him, and we share our last kisses and a long embrace.

"I'm afraid, Lalin," he says, "but with all the locks and window bars I believe I can't escape to harm anyone."

"I'll stay in the church when night falls, but as the moon rises, I plan to go home to make offerings to the saints and pray until dawn. You'll be safe. My saints will keep you. *Bondye a*nd my good magic work for us. Come let's look at all the locks."

We inspect the room. Bars on the windows look strong. When we try to pull on them, they won't bend or wobble. The bolt on the door is made of thick and heavy metal. Our priest has added padlocks on a bar across the door. When they're locked the entrance to the room will be even more secure.

It's hard for me to leave him there alone, but there's no choice for us.

I whisper all my love, as I close the door, locking with the heavy bolt. Dusk crowds the sunset clouds and deepens all the shades of crimson, pink and tangerine. The beauty of the evening contradicts the pain I feel.

Father Jules comes out and checks the padlocks on the door. He latches the shutters with another padlock. Grandmam waits for me, and we walk together along the banquette to enter through the Cathedral doors.

It's after midnight when we leave the sanctuary. Father insists to drive us home in his carriage. The moon gleams like a ginger-colored bubble. I swear I've never seen it shimmer with such a vibrant glow. I wonder does this have some meaning for us on this night. As our priest guides his horse around the corner from the Presbytere, I hear a ghostly howl rising from behind the building. The sound fills me with the shivers. I reach for Grandmam's hand.

As we pass the alleyway near our cathedral, I see a shadow bend around the corner. A howl to match the last one rises from that alley as we go by. Father slaps the reins across the horse's back and the carriage rumbles forward as it picks up speed.

Looking backwards, I see what I had feared. A hairy beast creeps along the building walls. I cover up my mouth to hold back a scream. Grandmam turns and sees it too.

"*Sacrebleu*! They'll try to get him out. What can we do?" she asks.

Father Jules leans forward and raps the reins to speed the horse. "I'll leave you off and turn back, so I can get some help. We'll find a way to beat them off before they can get to him."

"I only pray they can be stopped. We should have known they had a plan. First the monster bird and now the loup garou themselves. They do have a legendary strength." My words catch in my throat. The reality of my worst fears slinks towards the carriage house.

We reach Rue Burgundy. The carriage swerves around the corner. Grandmam and I cling to the edges of the seats to keep our balance. Only half a block until my house. Father reins in the horse to stop the carriage with a jerk at my door.

"There's no time to waste," he says and slides off the driver seat to help Grandmam down to the banquette. "Make strong prayers tonight," he calls, as he taps his stallion's back to rush on. The carriage lumbers forward, but gains speed as it rolls toward the corner.

Chapter Twenty-Nine

I had no sleep this night. All through the hours I dance in prayer circles. Grandmam Selene stays with me in my courtyard. She sings in her birdsong voice while I dance Calinda, pirouetting on my toes. Libations, I pour, on the stones. We make offerings. At last Erzulie comes to take control of me. With her powers on me, I have hope she means to help save Etienne from himself.

When my saint leaves me, I know what I must do. I tell Grandmam that I need to make the change to my feline self. Prayers and magic we made, but now I need to see what's happening at the priest's house. The full moon still glimmers in the sky. No sunrise comes for some hours.

* * *

Grandmam gives my feline self her blessing. She'll stay at my house all night, while I wander out to see for the better or the worse. I worry that the loup garou ranges through the Quarter. He may be just around the corner from the priest's home, where Etienne's locked in the carriage house to keep him contained during the full moon's phase.

I scurry down the banquette across Rue Toulouse and onward till I reach St. Ann. Here I pause, making sure my cat eyes are keen to catch sight of any shapes looming in the darkness. Carefully I proceed on my silent, padded paws. When I reach the Presbytere, I stop to listen for any sounds. No howls greet me, but I do hear whispers. Although the moon still offers some light in the sky, it has begun to sink below the rooftops. Darkness rules as I sneak through the gate into the courtyard. Two figures stand on the stones outside the carriage house. Yes, two men I see. Father Jules listens while the other fellow whispers.

Mon Dieu. What I realize is quite a huge surprise. Dr. Lycus Volcain raises up one hand and chops the air in front of Father Jules, while he speaks. I need to edge up closer to hear what he says.

"I told you Jules that my knowledge of the supernatural is quite extensive. I experienced a great deal through my study of these creatures and their magic. Of course, it's evil I admit, but it can be useful as I have demonstrated to you this night."

"But how did you do it? Did you see that they attacked me and shoved me down? I hit my head against the stones. I must have lost consciousness. When my senses came back, they were clamoring at the door, tearing away the boards with their claws. Then you appeared out of nowhere like a vision. I saw them turn to face you, growling, and I thought surely they would tear you to shreds, but instead they cowered..."

Dr. Lycus interrupts the priest. "Yes but, listen to me. You didn't see my weapon," he says. He holds up a silver derringer. "Let me check your head. Remember I am a doctor. You're hurt, Jules. I need to have a look."

Father rubs his head, but then stops and wags a finger at Lycus Volcain. "But why not shoot the monsters. They staggered back, then they slinked away with you stalking right behind them. I saw them climb the wall on the side of the carriage house."

"In truth, the pistol was loaded, but there were no silver bullets. Without those they can't be destroyed."

"Still they could be injured, if you fired at them."

Dr. Lycus shakes his head. "I knew that, but, at that moment, it seemed to me that would cause a scuffle. I thought you might need my help and decided that I should avoid a fight for your sake."

While I listen to these two, I try to visualize the scene that I just missed. My question is what was Dr. Lycus doing at the priest's home this time of night, but the answer to that question will have to wait. I won't reveal myself in my feline shape. I wait till later to shift to my human shape.

Father walks towards the carriage house to check the door. A few boards have been pulled off the hinges. When he checks the padlocks, I hear a low growl, almost a groan, coming from inside the room. Father listens at the door for several minutes then turns back to Lycus.

"It seems secure," he says and beckons to the doctor to follow him inside his house.

As much as I would truly like to hear the continuation of their conversation, I decide not to follow them. Perhaps I will look for an open window, but for now I want to check around the carriage house to see if I can learn anything of the loup garou attack. As I approach, I hear snarling sounds coming from behind the door. Surprising, I think that there's no scratching or beating on the door. Perhaps my loup garou has tired himself out before I arrived.

There is some damage to the shutters on the door. Pieces of the wood have been ripped off, but the locks have held. Standing near the door, I make a quiet meow. An eerie silence follows. Still I wait and meow again. Then the door rattles, a loud growl makes me jump backwards. The shutters shake with such a force that I hiss and feel my fur begin to bristle. Another silence continues for several minutes, then a low whimper begins. It grows louder and becomes a groan before it fades to nothing.

I'll wait here until sunrise. That's my plan. Then I'll find a place to hide and shift back to my woman self. Quietness dominates the courtyard, as I pad around to find a place to curl up for several hours. I'll try to sleep, but if I can't, I'll take the time to consider what our next moves should be.

* * *

I must have dozed, because when I open my eyes, the sun weaves patterns among the shadows on the courtyard stones. Streaks of light shine through the palm fronds. Everyone's still asleep inside the priest's house. Rising on my furry legs, I scamper to hide behind some oleanders. There I stretch out on a bed of leaves and pray for my change to come quickly. I feel my small body growing slowly. I close my eyes again and whisper prayers to St. Michael. Yes, he hears me because the paws are gone. My legs and arms come to me. Smooth skin replaces soft black fur, and my small pink nose and mouth melt to form my human features. At last I stand and rub my arms with my woman fingers. I stretch tall, standing on my toes. My muscles need this stretch. My feline body is lithe and supple, but when I shrink to cat-size the muscles have to shorten and grow tight. I take this time to bend and straighten, bend, and straighten until I feel like myself again.

Stepping out from behind courtyard shrubs, I know I need the keys to see my love and free him from his prison. So, I wait for Father Jules, who holds the keys. Although I have much patience for my healing practice, my tolerance for this wait grows thin. After some few minutes I trudge up to the priest's door and knock.

His maid, Geogette, comes and opens the door a crack. "Yes, Mamzelle, I hear Father walking on the floors upstairs, so he should be down in some few minutes. You wait here, and I will tell him."

She does not invite me in, but that's no surprise. She probably sees me as a problem for the priest and somehow extra work for her. She does leave the door half open, so that I can hear Father Jules coming down the steps. Voices mingle; I can't catch the words. It's not long until the door opens wide and our priest comes out to greet me.

His eyes look red from lack of sleep. He's not a young man. Most likely he has more than fifty years behind him. "Ah, Lalin," he says, "quite a long night for all of us. I know you are anxious for me to open up the door." He sighs and takes my hand. " You are a strong young woman, but you must prepare yourself for the worst. Your protector has had a hellish experience for many hours."

I nod and whisper a short prayer to our Holy Mother, as I follow him down the few steps into the courtyard. He takes out a ring of keys. While he begins to unbolt the door and open all the locks, I listen for sounds on the inside. First there's only silence, but then I notice a creak or two on the floorboards inside. There's footsteps.

Father gestures for me to stand back. His face's pinched with worry. All the locks have been released and the door slowly swings open. At first, I see nothing. Moving closer to the opening, I brush past Father to stand at the threshold.

"Lalin." Etienne calls my name.

I rush forward, but our priest holds me back. He steps in front of me. Now we both see my protector. He bends slightly forward, leaning up against the wall nearest to the door. His hair looks tangled, and clothes rumpled. Scratches cover his hands. Most of all his face shows a weariness that I've never seen before.

"My love," I cry out. At last Father Jules does not restrain me. Running forward, we fall together, our arms wrapped around each other. He staggers and I try to support his weight as best I can. He struggles to keep his balance and steady himself. I feel his body trembling.

"Let's get him into the Presbytere," Father says. "Here, lean on me, Etienne."

In the fresh air of the courtyard, my love breathes deeply. He stretches taller as if he's regaining some strength. "I had such a nightmare," he says. "Like nothing I could ever imagine."

We lead him up the few steps into the priest's home. Father calls his maid to bring out a pitcher of water, some rum and fresh clothing that I had brought for him last night. Into the parlor we go.

"Have a seat. Try to get comfortable. You don't have to talk now. A drink of rum will do you good." Father picks up a cushion from the sofa to give him a softer back to lean against.

Georgette brings in a tray with glasses and a decanter. Father pours a small glass of rum and hands it to my Etienne. "Drink this down and then have a glass of water. It's bound to help the stress that you're feeling."

Etienne takes the glass, drains it, then takes a second glass filled with water. He leans back against the chair and sighs so deeply that the fragrance of the rum floats up to me. He reaches for me now. I lean over him to give him one more hug.

"I saw blood flowing last night," he says. "Beasts with fangs and pointed claws. The growls were deafening and the screams even worse. I don't know where I was. All I know for sure is that I was surrounded by pain and suffering with no relief for any of it. I had to close my mind from the images. My sanity left me for that time."

Chapter Thirty

For two days my lover sleeps. I make a visit to his Papa's office to tell him Etienne has been ill. So it is that Monsieur Legendre comes to my home on Rue Burgundy to visit with his son. It is good, he says, that Etienne's mama is visiting family on a plantation outside the city. She would be much disturbed by the news of her son's illness.

Papa and my protector talk for almost an hour. I serve them coffee with chicory and a plate of calas, sweet rice cakes. Although I leave them to speak in private, I can hear the conversation. Etienne never mentions the loup garou or the curse that afflicts him. I suppose he's right to not alarm his papa, but I wonder if a time will come when he must reveal the truth.

***

It's quite late when Etienne wakes again. His conversation with his papa made him weary. I know he hates to hide the facts but feels he must. His family would be so upset by the frightening story.

"Let's enjoy a glass of wine, my love," I say to him and see him smile.

"Yes, yes, let's relax together, my Lalin."

We take our glasses through the French doors and out into my courtyard. I glance up at the moon, which still looks full to my eyes. It moves through its phases quicker than we can see. The total fullness lasts only for one night, if not less. I believe we are quite safe until the cycle completes again. This night brings cool breezes. Dazzling light from the glowing moon shines through the clouds, and stars like sparkling gems rise above the rooftops. A scent of jasmine blooming somewhere floats in the air.

Standing now in the center of my outdoor space, he takes me in his arms to give me one sweet kiss. Our lips melt together, tongues caressing. He leads me to my wrought iron bench, where we cuddle close. I feel the passion rising in him, but I wonder that he may need to release some painful tensions about what we had to face.

My guess is true. His arms slide slowly from me. He still leans close, but I see him wrestling with distressing thoughts. My hand he takes and holds on tight. "I find it's so difficult to describe what happened to me that night locked inside the carriage house." He stares down at our hands entwined together. "The transformation felt nothing like the shift that makes me be the ginger tabby."

We've placed our wine glasses on the stones beside the bench. He lifts his and takes a sip and offers me my glass. I touch mine to his to hear the crystal ring. He smiles, gives my hand a squeeze and then continues. "The changes to my body felt like bones breaking and bending in a painful twisting fashion. My head seemed to nearly burst with jaws and fangs that I couldn't see but knew were there. Hair bristled out my pores. My hands and feet grew full of claws. Lying on the floor I had no control once it all began..." He pauses, shakes his head, and looks at me. He squints like the effort to recall has caused a fog to cloud his vision.

"If you'd rather not tell more, I understand," I say. "It's as you wish, my love. I'm not asking."

His hand tightens on my fingers so hard that I almost cry out. Then he releases my hand and clasps his together. "Well, the worst came after that. I lost my brain. My stomach churned. I crawled along the floor. At the door I stood again and raked claws across the boards in all directions. Harshness rumbled in my throat. So strange! Then howls came from all around me. I couldn't see what was there." He hesitates, coughs in his hands, and begins to gag. Long breaths he takes.

"Then it happened like a dream. I saw the loup garou scrambling through the trees somewhere. It looked like a place I'd been before. Suddenly there were people all around, screaming. Then the blood, the blood..." He stops, covers his face with both hands. He rises with a jerk, but then slumps back against the iron railing of the bench. "It's all a blur after that. I can't remember."

"That's enough," I say. "You're putting yourself through all the pain again." This time I pick up his glass of wine. "Here, have a sip, and then try to clear your mind. It's too much horror to relive that night again."

He listens to me, taking several swallows of the wine. His eyes close. We sit in silence. A cricket chirps somewhere in my courtyard flower beds of golden bells and sweet pink camellias. It's time for us to go inside. Where are the happy thoughts I need? So much stress I feel for him. How can I give some relief? I search my mind for ways to take him back to passion and away from all the nightmares.

Chapter Thirty-One

We finished one whole bottle of rich red wine last night. And I confess I mixed a special potion in our last two glasses. Etienne didn't see me sprinkle powders in the goblets. The potion wipes away the stressful thoughts. It intensifies the passion that comes to us through our kisses and caresses. In this way we retire to my boudoir filled with love and the need to come together.

* * *

My protector returns to the shipping office early this morning. He's regained his full strength he tells me. I worry for him, but his face has a brighter look. His shoulders, I massage, while he sips his coffee. My hands tighten on the knots around his muscles. At last the stiffness loosens.

When he rises and takes a waistcoat from the rack, I help him button up to face a chilly breeze outside. We kiss good-bye. He whispers love words in my ear and gives his best smile. "*Merci, mon cher.* I'll see you after work is done."

Even as I'm basking with relief that evilness has passed for a time, I know that I must begin to work out a plan to rid ourselves of the curse. I have some thoughts on what my next moves will be. First a visit to see Grandmam Selene. She may want to accompany me to speak with Father Jules. He mentioned that he discovered information that should help to break the spell.

It's still early when I lock my doors and begin my walk down Rue Burgundy. Sunlight penetrates the clouds that wrap around the sky this morning. A silver whiteness gives the day a sparkle even as the haze drifts above this Quarter of the city.

As I pass the corner of Toulouse, I see a woman at the other end of that block. She wears a shawl I recognize. When she sees me, she waves, and I realize that my friend, Apolline, is walking towards me.

She calls out, "Lalin, so good to see you."

I stop to wait for her to reach me. She's almost running. Her tignon loosens and nearly flies off her head, so she pauses for a moment to tie it tight.

"I thought I'd drop by your house to see you this morning. It's been quite some time. We need to talk." From the way she smiles now, I know she brings cheer and no sad tales.

"So, all's well with you, *mon amie*. It's good to see you too."

"Ah, I've not been bothered by my enemies, Abel and friends of late. I hope your life has been going well," she says.

I hesitate to tell her about all the grief and frustration, but, on the other hand, it occurs to me that she may offer some assistance. I know she would be willing. We've formed a trusting friendship in our time together.

"There's been difficult times of late, Apolline. I go now to meet with Grandmam Selene and then to the Presbytere to see the Father Jules."

Her eyes grow wide. "It's not trouble with the loup garou I hope," she says. And I wonder to myself if she can read my mind.

"Yes, much trouble with those shifters." I shake my head and draw a deep breath. My emotions are in control but seeing my friend staring at me now with such a worried look, brings all the sadness back.

"How can I help?" she asks.

I make a quick decision. Yes, I will confide in her. "If you have the time before going to the market, you can come with me. I can tell the story as we walk along, and you'll hear more detail and opinion from my grandmam and especially from Father Jules."

Apolline agrees, and we proceed to Rue St. Ann to visit Grandmam Selene. She listens as I do my best to give her a clear account of what has happened to Etienne. Her face changes as I explain. She looks almost sick when I tell her about the curse and what my Etienne has suffered only one day ago. Her own experiences with the Arachne spell must haunt her still. Tears slide down her cheeks. She pulls a handkerchief from a pocket and wipes her face. Her lips are twisted in a frown.

"Oh, Lalin, so awful to hear all this. Somehow this evil must end."

"I'm grateful that we do have Father Jules to help us. The city police offer no aid at all. We are on our own to find the cure for him. And keep the shifters away while we do."

We've nearly reached the intersection with St. Ann. As we step from the banquette to cross, one carriage turns the corner so sharply that I grab Apolline's arm to pull her back. It came so close to us that I felt a rush of air between the coach and my body. I look to see the driver, but his face is turned the other way. I say nothing of it but wonder if it was our enemies out to knock me down in the middle of the road.

In minutes we enter through Grandmam's gate and stroll to her front door. She's dressed for the day and, although she wants us to sit down for some refreshments, I tell her that we should carry on, to meet with our priest to learn what we can about the ways to cure my darling, Etienne.

Apolline and I make an extra effort to tie Grandmam's tignon into a fashionable shape. I help her with her cloak, and we're on our way again. Several Creole gentlemen pass us on the banquette as we continue. Many of these fellows can come late to their offices it seems. They are dressed in fine waistcoats and silk top hats that gleam in the rays of sunlight.

We reach the Presbytere where Father Jules resides. His servant girl, Geogette, tells us that we can find him at the Cathedral. Mass has ended, but he's not yet returned. As we walk, we see our priest standing on the steps, speaking to some of his most loyal parishioners. Father nods and listens, while several older Creole ladies stand beside him talking. We wait for him at the bottom of the steps.

Our priest usually smiles; he's generally a cheerful man of God. But lately his face shows stress. He's been affected by our misfortune almost as much as me and Etienne. He walks towards us and greets us with a serious tone.

"*Bonjour*," he says. I quickly introduce him to Apolline, but they agree they've met before, although she admits she doesn't attend Mass as often as she should.

Father invites us to accompany him to his residence. He says that what he's learned should help us to decide what methods to use to save Etienne from his misfortune. In the parlor of his house, we settle ourselves for discussion. Grandmam and Apolline sit on a plush sofa near the fireplace, while Father and I sit side by side in high-back chairs across from them.

"Although it's written that the curse will last no less than 101 days, I've found several remedies in the occult texts that we must study for any exorcism. It's possible to rid him of the onus even before the time is up."

"So, it's true the curse must last at least that number of days?" I ask.

"Yes, it can in fact last a lifetime. It's a frightful thing we're dealing with. The most successful cases for a cure involve a blood exchange."

Apolline gasps out loud at his statement. I turn to her and then to Grandmam. We all exchange these looks for several seconds. And then our priest begins to speak again.

"It's not a happy thing, but it's the best I've been able to uncover. If we somehow get blood from Etienne during his transformation to the loup garou, it can be passed on to another person." He clears his throat and then continues. "Of course, we're not likely to find a volunteer to take on the loup garou curse. But I had one thought that might..."

I interrupt him. I understand or perhaps I've read his mind without intention. "Yes, of course, you're thinking I could take the curse on myself."

"No, no, no..." Apolline cries out.

I am so startled by her outburst that my breath catches in my throat and comes puffing out with a cough. Grandmam winces and Father shakes his head.

But I hold my hand up with a straight arm. "Wait, Apolline! Let me explain. As a mambo with my magic, I should be able to destroy the spell. Between Grandmam and myself, we'll surely find the solution. Remember, after all, we were able to get the answers needed to lift the Arachne curse from you."

Father Jules nods. "You have stated almost exactly my thoughts on the matter. I hated to suggest it, but it's hard to think of how else a transfer could be made. As a priest, I could not condone putting such an onus on another parish person. Still this method offers dangers to you, Lalin. There may be problems solving such a horror."

"It's a risk that I must take. I believe my magic and the saints will bring me through it."

Chapter Thirty-Two

And so, Etienne and I must work out a plan. We'll need assistance no doubt, but it's mostly between the two of us. That's where the risks and responsibilities rest. He's quite against my proposal. I have no commitment from him to follow through. He balks at the idea that I would take on the curse to make him free again. I spend hours explaining how between Grandmam and me, there's no chance that I will be suffering for long. With our charms and potions, we will be able to breakdown the evil.

Our discussions have continued for two weeks. Time passes quickly, so I have barely fourteen days left to convince him if we want to try the remedy at the next full moon. Although neither of us expresses anger, the tension interrupts our love life.

This morning as we drink our coffee, he says to me, "Lalin, I can't agree to this scheme. We can find another way. I love you too much to allow you to put yourself in so much danger."

I say nothing. There's no point in arguing, and I can understand his fears. While I sit in silence, he rises from his chair to come to me. Gently he pulls me up from my seat and kisses me. I feel his heartbeat in rhythm with mine. He holds me tight, then stepping back he caresses my shoulders, and runs his hands along my hips.

"We can't lose our love, *mon cher*. Without you, my life has no meaning. A plan like that could destroy us"

I must give up. He has reason for his fears. For this time, I smile and let the subject go, but it's not forgotten. We need a chance to express our passion.

* * *

As the week's end approaches, I try to forget the worries for this day. Etienne has left for work. I decide to walk to the market to purchase fresh fish for our supper. While I'm there I'll look for Apolline. She's a comfort to me now.

On Saturday night she'll come with me to the Bayou St. John to meet with my people. I've not had the gathering with them, since before that last full moon. We'll make plans, she and I. My magic and my healing I"ve neglected. It's time for me to help my followers again. St. Michael and Erzulie will join me on that evening.

I'm in luck to find my friend at her stall, selling gris-gris and charms to Creole ladies and even some Creole men. The men try to make sure that no one sees them purchasing these items at the market. Apolline and I laugh at them when they walk away. It's funny to see them looking all around the vendors, as if they'd like to find a place to hide.

It feels good to laugh again. Apolline and I talk about the meeting and I tell her that I'll contact my assistants, the men who help us build the fire and handle the snake for me. The serpent I must hold above my head to remind the crowd that I am the queen. I'll show humbleness but still I maintain my power. The healing's most important. Charms and herbal potions help me to relieve problems with romance, sadness and even anger. And, so we make our plans to meet at my house on Rue Burgundy this Saturday after dark.

✶ ✶ ✶

A chill descends as the sun slips down behind the houses in our Vieux Carre. I love this time of day. The clouds frame the sky in pastel shades, setting off the wash of dusky blues. Soon a cloak of indigo spreads across the wide stretch of paler blues. Night comes to drape itself around us. From the heavens, stars begin to sprinkle light. This canvas hangs above our meeting place on the banks of Bayou St. John.

Etienne must work late at his office, so I left his supper on the table, making sure it's covered to keep it warm for him. I hired a carriage to take Apolline and me to the bayou road. Luckily, the driver lives near her. When I hear the knock at my door, I know that they arrived. With my warmest cloak tied around my shoulders, I step out onto the banquette to greet my friend.

Apolline wears the white cotton blouse I made for her and her long full skirt a slightly deeper shade of blue than mine. I tell her that this meeting will be a most important one. My spirits give an inkling of the consequence. The vision isn't clear, but there's some fresh idea or knowledge coming to us. She listens intently as we turn now onto the bayou road. Ahead of us there's a flash of light among the giant oaks and cypress trees. Soon we see the bonfire in the distance. Gray smoke swirls in circles, rising through the trees.

A large crowd is waiting. Some sit on the ground on raggedy coverlets, while others stand in groups around the fire. Our driver slows the carriage. My men approach to help us down from our carriage seats.

Someone in the crowd calls out, "She's here. The queen arrived!"

Three drummers, spaced around the bonfire in the distance, begin to beat their rhythm. Some followers begin to sing in Creole French:

Eh, Yé, Yé Mamzelle,
Ya, yé, yé,li konin tou, gris-gris
Li, ti, kowri, avec vieux kikordi;
Oh, yé Mamzelle Lalin. . .

Their voices rise as we proceed toward the fire. "Grand Zombi," they sing, as one of my followers brings out the wooden box that holds the serpent. Perhaps six women begin to circle, swaying arms and hips as they move around the man who holds the Zombi's box.

"Danse Calinda," they sing out. These women begin to bend forward turning slowly. Their bodies undulate to the rhythm of the drums.

Before I even reach the center of the crowd, I feel the spirits all around me. My most beautiful Erzulie, she's like the Queen of Heaven, comes towards me. I can see her spirit-shape weaving through nearby trees. Among the tangled threads of Spanish moss, she twirls and twists. Ah, I feel her on me now. She rides me. I rise on my toes, spinning, spinning . My people step back to make a space for me to dance.

My man, Andre, with the Zombi's box, strides toward me. He opens the box, standing near the bonfire and lifts it high above his head.

"The Zombi, the great Zombi," he cries out, and many followers echo his words.

Andre lowers the box in front of me. My consciousness returns to me. I still dislike this snake. A deep breath, I take, to calm my fears before I reach into the serpent's home. The smooth skin I feel as I lift this creature. Its black eyes stare down at me when I raise it high above my head. It slithers down my arm, sliding to my shoulder.

"Erzulie," I whisper to her, "please give me all the strength I need to do this."

Ah, she sends me power now. "Your Queen is here," I call out, but this is her voice not mine. I glide and pirouette around the bonfire, while the serpent dangles from my shoulders. I still see Apolline at my side. Many people join our dance as we prance to the lively pulsing of the drums. My body grows looser; I bend backwards, arms weaving through the air. When at last I sink to the ground, Andre wrestles with the snake to make sure it's returned to the wooden box.

Erzulie's starting to retreat, but before she goes, I have a sign from her. While I'm lying on the ground, I hear a sound. A horse's hooves. Yes, I'm sure of it, but when I open my eyes there's no horse. It's like a vision in my ears.

I rise and see that Andre has brought me a small stool to sit on. He hands me a rosary. Apolline appears at my side with a satchel full of herbs and potions. The crowd grows quiet. It's time for healing to begin. So many familiar faces and yet I see a few that come for the first time. Some of my people hum a song in Creole French. I raise my hands and beckon to my followers to come forward to seek advice and remedies for all complaints and problems. They know I do my best to bring solutions.

One sweet woman named Marthe walks toward me bowing from her waist. "No need for that," I say and extend my hand to welcome her to come closer.

"Ah, Mamzelle," she whispers, "I have pains in my hands and sometimes elbows too. It's so hard for me to do my work with all the aching."

"Show me your hands," I say to her. When she holds out her arms, I see knobs around her knuckles. It's what we call polyarthrite with the joints and muscles. "Let me give you this." I take out some peppermint oil I have made from the leaves and a small bag with some aloe.

She listens while I tell her how to make the medicine that will help her with her pains. With hot towels to help the inflammation, she should get some relief.

"*Merci,* Mamzelle," she says, "I'll bring you bags of fresh vegetables from my garden to pay for all your help.

We exchange a warm embrace before she moves away. The next patient steps up and kneels in front of me. Many have come tonight to seek treatments. There are some who need advice concerning family problems. Soon several hours pass. After all this time sitting on this small low stool, I need to stand to stretch my legs. I bring prayer hands to lips and close my eyes for one whole minute. When I open them again, I find a big surprise standing tall and elegant in front of me.

"Monsieur Volcain, Dr. Lycus..." I blurt out.

"Mademoiselle Lalin." He tips his hat, gives me his always charming smile.

"You certainly surprise me."

"I must apologize then for startling you. I should have made a contact sooner. In fact, I had intended to send a note to advise you that I planned to come tonight."

Standing behind my impressive friend, several people wait to see me with their problems. "Dr. Lycus," I say," did you have a matter to discuss with me?"

Now he sees that I have a few more people waiting for me. "Ah, yes, we need to talk, but I'll wait until you finish with your healing work."

When the last of my people have come to seek my help. I see my acquaintance waits nearby. He's speaking to Apolline. She seems entranced. He uses all his charms with her, but that's his way.

Ah, for the moment I had almost forgotten about his presence at the carriage house on the full moon. Why was he there? When I asked Father Jules what happened with Dr. Lycus and the loup garou, he described the scene that I myself observed. His exact words, as I remember, were, *Lycus has occult knowledge of these shapeshifters. From what he tells me, it seems he may have handled some of them in his practice. He mentioned that he can offer help.*

What is it that makes this man such a mystery? I can never see into his mind. My saints maintain a silence when I seek the answers. Now he comes towards me with Apolline stepping just behind him. "*Mon cher*, Lalin," he calls, so familiar with his endearing terms. "At last we can speak together."

"Ah, yes, how may I help you, Dr. Lycus?"

"You know I've always had a sense about you. Your Etienne has great troubles in these recent days. I feel it's time that I step forward to offer help." There's no smile now. His lips curve down. He tilts his head to one side, as if he analyzes me with care.

"Father Jules did tell me that you offered your assistance. We're working on a plan to rid Etienne of this curse. Father's readings showed us an antidote."

Lycus stands in silence for such a long time that I begin to wonder if he heard me. Finally, he replies, "Yes, I believe that you'll consider a blood transfer. Am I correct?" He puckers up his lips and with a tightened brow he looks straight into my eyes.

"I don't know where you heard that, but it has been considered. Of course, we have to wait until the moon comes full again."

"Indeed, Jules has hinted at the possibility, but I believe like him that it's much too risky for you to attempt what you're planning to..."

I must interrupt him even though I've given up on that solution. Etienne has vowed that he's totally against it, and I must give in to his strong admonishment. Still, Dr. Lycus doesn't have to know. And I do want to hear what he has to say about the scheme.

"My magic's strong enough to give me powers that I need. And, with Grandmam Selene to back me up, I believe it's the best chance we have to rid ourselves of this curse." Now I stop talking and wait for him to speak.

He stares at me. "But why put yourself in danger. Why not find a culprit to take the curse? There must be someone that you'd like to pass it to. Surely you can name a guilty party."

Can he be serious? What an evil thought to put it on to someone else. I turn to Apolline, who nods as if she agrees with him. The image of a face flashes in my mind. "I never thought of it. It seems so cruel."

Mon Dieu, his lips curve in a smile again. Can he read my mind? I have enemies for sure. One I can picture, although there are at least two others who have done me wrong.

The three of us stand near the dying bonfire. A silence falls that lasts while we watch the flickers of the embers. The last of my people walk to their wagons or hurry to catch a ride in someone's skiff along the bayou. Andre approaches to ask if I need him to help me before he takes off in his own wagon. I thank him and wish him well for his ride home.

Dr. Lycus still waits for me to speak, so I begin. "It's true I have thought of three people, who've threatened me. Two of them are awaiting trial, but one is free. A woman always ready to do me harm. She's also been a danger to my Etienne."

"Yes, you see I knew there would be someone. So, you can take the danger from yourself."

"Indeed, I could be glad to punish that woman with the loup garou curse. But how to mix his blood with hers? I don't know if it's possible." I close my eyes for a moment and see the plump Yvette with her pretty dress and curly hairdo.

When I look at Lycus Volcain again, his smile brightens to fill his face. He looks so pleased. "I'm sure that I can help with this. Ask Jules if you have doubts. He knows that I have the experience needed."

Chapter Thirty-Three

Today I meet with Father Jules and Dr. Lycus. So far, I've not mentioned this to Etienne. Could we really pass the curse to someone? Dr. Lycus hasn't given any details of a plan. Although I sent a note to our priest, I left it to Lycus to speak to him. It seems unlikely that Father will agree to this plan. I've not told Grandmam about his suggestion. This morning I'll let her know what I'm thinking of. I'll also tell Apolline so that she may join us if she wishes. It's possible that we can use her help.

Etienne leaves early for his office, so I make myself ready for the day. As soon as the morning dishes are washed and stored away, I'm off to meet with Grandmam Selene. My thoughts have me in a daze, as I walk fast towards Rue St. Ann. When I turn the corner to get to Grandmam's, what I see makes me stop in mid-step.

Lycus Volcain stands on the opposite side of this intersection. It's who he's speaking with that alarms me. The handsome profile's clear. Abel, the loup garou, faces Dr. Lycus. I move quick into the open entry of a carriage gate. Hidden from their view, I watch. I pray my saints would let me hear the conversation, but I can only view their gestures.

Abel claps his hands together, then pats Lycus on the back. Lycus reaches forward to grasp the other man's shoulder, leaning in as if he whispers something in his ear. After that he turns his palms up to the sky and shakes his head. When they finally part, I find a lump of air's caught in my throat. Still I watch as the doctor continues down Rue St. Ann towards the priest's house, and Abel rounds the corner and stops to hail a carriage on Rue Burgundy.

It seems these two are friends. And I've only just begun to trust Lycus Volcain. This can't be good news for me. I walk slowly down the block to reach my grandmam's house. What decision should I make? If I confront him now, it disrupts the current meeting. My inclination is to hold my tongue and wait. There's no one to consult with on this matter. Meanwhile I will see what images my magic can offer me. For now, I'll keep this news to myself.

* * *

Grandmam and I sit together on Father's sofa. Dr. Lycus sits across from us in a high back chair. Father Jules comes in from the hallway. In his arms are stacks of books. They appear to be the ancient texts that he said he found in a storeroom of the Presbytere.

"Here we have the works that I've discovered. There's descriptions of the occult and rituals involving demons and such as that." He plops the books onto the rectangular wooden table that sits in front of us.

Grandmam reaches for one book, which is bound in black leather. Under that one, I see a thicker volume. The binding's frayed at the corners but the title on the front remains readable. "The Necromancer's Manuscript."

As I'm about to reach for this manual, our priest picks it up and begins to turn through the pages. "Ah, here it is," he says, and hands the book to Lycus instead of me.

I say nothing to any of them about seeing Dr. Lycus at the corner. There's truly danger there, but I need to consult my saints before I pass on this information or confront him. While I'm thinking to myself, Grandmam shows me a description in the pages she's been leafing through. She jabs a finger at one paragraph.

The words explain a ritual for removing demonic spells. But these descriptions require an exorcism. Father Jules hasn't mentioned a ritual as a solution for my Etienne. While I'm reading all the details, Dr. Lycus looks up from "The Necromancer's Manuscript" he's been reading. He motions to our priest to have a look at one yellowed page near the middle of the book.

"Look here! I believe this may work to save Etienne from this evil, Jules."

Father takes the book from him, squinting at the faded print. But then he shakes his head. "Yes, I know there are several accounts of these exorcisms. I read about it in other texts. But I found no record of success for the loup garou curse."

Lycus nods, as if he agrees, but then continues. "This one's different. It does involve a bloodletting."

"Let me see it." Father and I say these words at the same time.

A smile spreads across our friend's face. "Study it," he says. "I'm not a religious man myself. In fact, I avoid the Mass. Forgive me, Jules, but after all we're old school friends, and you understand that I have lost faith. Don't hold that against me."

Father sighs. "Lycus, I accept you as you are, although I always hope to change your feelings for the church. At one time you were a believer."

"It's all like nonsense to me. However, this requires the training of your faith. My beliefs are secondary. We must see if these ancient rituals have some potential. Indeed, you may put your expertise to work."

I must admit this fellow is persuasive. His voice has some hypnotic effect.

Father opens the book again, pulls up a chair and begins to read the pages. I watch his face most carefully, and I see Grandmam do the same. Lycus picks up another treatise from the table, turning through the pages. We all keep silent, waiting to see what the priest will say.

At last he looks up from the book. "You're correct this ritual's quite unusual. The blood must be taken when the person in his demon shape. That, of course, makes the ceremony difficult to achieve."

"Wait, let me see that again." Dr. Lycus reaches for the book.

Father passes it back to him, indicating the paragraph that he's been reading. Again, we watch as Lycus narrows his eyes and turns the page. After perhaps one minute he looks up.

"But here we have an alternative." He reads a passage from the new page. "If the victim still alternates between the human and the demonic form, the ritual remains basically the same. The deviation that is made in this case will be that the blood will be used to mark a cross on the forehead of the victim. Crosses must also be marked on the palm of each hand."

Our priest nibbles at his lower lip. "Well, it seems this may be our best hope of ridding Etienne of this menace."

The discussion turns to the time of the next full moon. Grandmam knows the exact date, and Father Jules notes it on his calendar. As I listen to them talk, I begin to feel light-headed, and my heartbeat slows. Ah, the familiar presence of my Erzulie comes to me. She brings me dreams.

While the others continue their conversation, I close my eyes. At first there's only darkness. Then my saint brings pictures. In this vision I see Lycus riding on his stallion. The scene's like our first meeting, when Etienne and I were on the bayou road. The fog flows all around us. But I'm just an observer there.

The loup-garou cottage in the woods comes into view. The doctor dismounts and goes to the door. Ah, yes, he's greeted by our enemies. In fact, they appear to be quite impressed with him. His cape swirls around him while he removes his black top hat. Yvette takes the hat, Abel helps him with his cloak, and they all gather around the table in the center of the room.

"The Master's here; the Master's here." These are the only words I hear.

My body shakes, so hard my teeth rattle in my ears. The room begins to spin. Erzulie's on me now. She rides me. An image of Yvette dominates the vision. Fire comes up from somewhere. I feel the heat. Yes, it grows too hot. I don't know what's happening. I can hardly breath, but still the vision enfolds around me.

The loup garou circle Yvette. Where's the Dr. Lycus? I don't see him. I float above this scene. Ah, there he is, standing near the door completely still. I don't know what this means. Yvette slides away from my view, but then I see a giant hawk soaring near the ceiling above the wolf men. It swoops and perches on the doctor's shoulder. It's beak grazes at his earlobe.

In one quick move, he grasps the bird with both hands. Some feathers fly. He holds on for a moment but then he releases it and opens the door. The wind gusts through. The hawk's caught in the surge. The flames flash all around. I feel my body sinking. Erzulie's with me still. We fall into the dark, swirling, circling in something like a whirlpool, and yet wrapped in a blanket of the blackest night.

Chapter Thirty-Four

Coolness against my face. The next thing I remember I'm lying on the floor. Grandmam wipes my cheeks with a wet cloth. Father Jules bends over me reading something from his prayer book. Lycus, I don't see.

I feel weak. Erzulie left me. I go almost lifeless after that, but slowly my mind comes back to me. I try to sit up. Grandmam holds me down against the floor. "It's too soon," she says. "You must take your time to get up, Lalin. Your body shakes so hard that you need to gain some strength back before you move."

She's right I know, but still my main wish is to get up and collect my thoughts about the meaning of the vision. Now I see Dr. Lycus come up from behind our priest. He carries something in his hand. Ah, a sponge, he says. Full of vinegar from the strong smell of it. Funny, I think that this doctor thought to revive me with vinegar.

"Ah, good, she's awake." He smiles at me. "I was concerned. Your pulse rate gave us quite a panic."

"I'll be fine. Perhaps a glass of water would be good though." Grandmam nods and Father goes off to fetch the glass. My grandmam's the only one who understands what happened. She knows there's been a vision. But neither of us will give this explanation to Father Jules. Dr. Lycus may suspect what happened as he's more attuned to magic and the effects that it may bring about. But the powers of my saints are something that he doesn't recognize. He's well-informed on the occult; religion remains a distant concept like a relic from his childhood.

Our priest returns with a glass of water, and I sit up and take it from him. While I sip, I try to recall the dream that Erzulie sent me. The loup garou greeted Lycus with respect. But it's what happened with the giant bird that puzzles me. If the vision had just lasted long enough for me to see. From what

I remember the hawk was caught up in a gust of wind. Dr. Lycus released it. Fire, yes, there were flames licking all around that cottage room. Yes, and fire's the greatest fear for the loup garou.

My eyes follow this man around the room. Father Jules asks me questions, but I only shake my head. Lycus pauses at the edge of the fireplace and steps back with a slight jerk. Father turns from me to his friend.

"If you feel a chill, feel free to light a fire," he says.

I note his eyes grow wide, eyebrows lifted. "No, no…," the doctor says, but quickly pauses, and continues in a softer voice. "It's quite warm in here without a fire, Jules."

I try to catch his eye, but he moves away from the hearth. He turns his brightest smile towards us now. "Well, I believe our Lalin needs time to recover from her fainting spell. We should plan to meet again soon to work out all details of the ritual to cure Etienne of his curse."

Father immediately agrees with him before I have time to make any objections. Grandmam still hovers over me, so I know that my protest would not be taken seriously.

Our priest looks at the calendar. Another date is set for a meeting. Lycus retrieves his hat and cape, wishes us well and goes on his way. Grandmam and I remain with Father. I take the time now to explain that I had visions from my saint. Although I describe the creatures in the dream, I don't name Lycus as the central figure. Father purses his lips and sighs. I know he finds my magic goes against all his religious teachings.

Grandmam Selene and I discuss the next meeting date with him. We decide to meet first in the church to pray, and then go to the Presbytere. Father escorts us to the door.

"Please call me if anything happens with Etienne. This situation has been troubling me for some time. I also have concerns for Monsieur and Madame Legendre, who clearly know nothing of this awful malady."

"Thank you, Father, for all your help. As for Etienne's parents, there's really nothing they can do to help. No need to bring them more worries." I say nothing else. But in fact, Etienne maintains that his strongest wish is to leave his parents out of his dilemma. He's worried that there's a weakness in his mama's heart.

Beyond my fears for Etienne, I have one main concern. How can I discover this connection between Dr. Lycus and Abel, the loup garou? With only days now until the full moon rises, I must use my shape-shifting to follow and observe this fellow. If only my saints would give me a clearer vision of what this man really stands for. Does he have a fear of fire? I recall how he reacted when Father Jules mentioned building fire in the hearth. His response seemed a bit extreme.

So, it is this morning that I decide to take my feline self around our Quarter to see what I can find about Lycus Volcain. As soon as my protector leaves for work, I clear up the plates and prepare for my transformation. My magic comes to me quickly, and I am blessed with my furry self within a few minutes.

Through the French doors I saunter and pad my way across the courtyard to the oak tree. Up I climb, leaping to the roof of the kitchen room. Scampering over tiles, I go to Rue Toulouse, managing to edge my way to a nearby alley. From there I jump onto a pile of wooden boxes. They topple over, but I avoid collision. At last I'm on the banquette and ready to explore the Vieux Carre. I take my time. It's still early. Surely, I can find my acquaintance before the day is over.

My first plan is to travel to the Place d'Armes. From there the market's only a short distance. If I have luck, Dr. Lycus may be there to do some shopping. Rue Royal has some coffee shops I can roam around. It's true that the Quarter has many streets for my small cat feet to cover; still I believe I have a chance of finding him today.

Some hours later my paws grow weary from all the walking. My feline nature catches me. I can't resist a nap. As I'm about to curl up inside an open courtyard entrance, I hear the familiar voice I've been searching for.

He's with another gentleman that I've not seen before. They stroll past the courtyard entrance where I now hide behind a potted palm. It may be difficult for me to follow undetected, still that's a risk I must take. Creeping on my furry feet, I slink close against the walls of buildings, sliding into doorways where I can. At one corner they pause, and I am close enough to hear the conversation.

Dr. Lycus has some business with this gentleman. The man carries a leather satchel like the local doctors. It seems likely that he's a medical man. But I've never seen him before. His speech is clearly from the old country. And then I understand why this is. They're discussing a trip to France.

"I must return soon," Lycus says. "I have work to complete at home. It's been a good trip for me, and I believe I've found a cure."

My ears stand straight up when I hear these words. I pray my saints will let me hear more of this conversation. But then a noisy carriage rumbles by and I miss his next words. I edge closer, hiding behind a broken shutter that hangs on the wall behind him.

This time the other man speaks. "Your problem is certainly unique. I'd never guess you had such an affliction."

"I thought you knew of my family. Many from our region know the history. The Dukedom of the Volcain dynasty has been plagued for generations."

The two men have reached a cafe along Rue Royal. They pause to read a menu posted near the door. Lycus nods, and they pass through the entrance. I inch along the buildings wall, hoping to sneak in behind them, but, when I try to creep across the threshold, a concierge spies me and grabs a walking stick to shake at me.

Although I wait for some time, I grow too tired to stay until they come out again. At last I give up for this day and make my way home.

Chapter Thirty-Five

In my house again, I shift to my human shape, and begin to prepare a dinner for my Etienne. As I add some spices to the stew, I cook for him, I consider what I have learned this day. Two important things for me to ponder run through my mind, while I begin to boil the water for the rice. First the Dr. Lycus says he will return to his home in France. I wonder how soon he leaves. What of his intent to assist with Etienne and his malady? Then there's his statement about finding a cure with the implication that he has some problem of his own. The words that stand out in my mind are: *The Dukedom of the Volcain dynasty has been plagued for generations.*

So, it is that I spend my cooking time wishing there had been some way to follow the two men and listen to the rest of their conversation.

An hour later my small dining table is set with bowls, plates, and silverware. While I place the wine glasses on the buffet, I hear Etienne come in the front door. With only a few days now before the fullness of the moon, I read the tension in his demeanor. He removes his jacket then he comes to kiss me.

"The food smells wonderful, Lalin," he says. But his voice sounds flat without the happiness he usually shows when he first sees me in the evening. There's no smile. He shrugs, pulls out a dining chair, and almost flops onto the cushioned seat.

I pour him a full glass of dark red wine. Before I present it to him though, I move to return his kiss with a long caress. Standing up again, he lowers his head against my shoulder, and I feel his sadness. For now, I decide to spare him the latest words I've heard from Dr. Lycus. These new bits of information I'll share with my grandmam instead.

* * *

When I tell Grandmam Selene about what I overheard from Dr. Lycus, she says we should go to Father Jules to ask about the meaning. If it's true that they have known each other for many years, then it seems likely that the priest knows more about the past than he has mentioned.

The early Mass has ended and so we think to catch him while he's free. He will listen to confessions in the afternoon, so this morning should be a good time. We go together to the rectory. Father comes to the door himself when we knock. Then I tell him that Grandmam Selene and I have some questions for him, and he nods and invites us in. As he leads us into his sitting room, I begin my explanation for our call.

"I apologize for this unexpected visit, Father, but yesterday I heard some surprising news. Since it may relate to Etienne and the cures we've discovered, I want to know what you think of it."

Our priest raises eyebrows with surprise or curiosity. "I'm glad to help, but what news relates to me?"

"In my feline form, I overheard a conversation between Lycus Volcain and another Frenchman. Two things mentioned caused me to wonder about the man's honesty." As I continue, Father Jules pulls up a chair for my grandmam. I follow but remain standing. "First, he said he's planning to return to France quite soon, which I found surprising. And then he spoke of an affliction that has plagued his family for generations. We thought that you might know something of this."

Father crosses his arms over his chest and tips his chin up as if he's looking at the ceiling. When he faces us again, he speaks slowly, "I am aware that Lycus plans to return to France before the summer comes, but I've not heard him speak of dates." He closes his eyes now, as if he's thinking hard.

"An affliction that's plagued his family does take me back to some years ago. I believe that some family members were badly affected by physical or possibly mental problems. His ancestors, of course, had their connections to the royal family, so genetic flaws did occur."

"Do you know what kind of problems?" I ask.

"Lycus never discussed the specifics, but some relatives were confined to the family estate. Rumors of madness were sometimes circulated in the nearby village. But family secrets can make for strange tales, as I'm sure you know."

"How strange." I turn to Grandmam, who looks as puzzled as I feel. Still I ask about his taking leave. "Do you think he'll be sailing soon? My impression was he planned to assist us in our efforts to break the spell on Etienne."

"Yes, in fact I spoke to him again the other day about the things we had discussed."

Grandmam nods and rises from the chair. "You seem to feel a confidence in the man, Father. Lalin doubts of his good character."

I hesitate, but it's clearly time for me to tell them what I saw between Lycus and Abel. "There's something else," I say. "Yesterday I did a search for him in my feline form, because of what I'd seen the day before."

Father Jules and Grandmam Selene both turn to face me.

"When I was on my way to your house on St. Ann, I saw Dr. Lycus at the corner before I turned. But what a surprise I had when I recognized the man he greeted on the banquette. I stepped into a courtyard entrance, so they didn't see me. The other man was Abel, the loup garou."

Grandmam stares wide-eyed at me. Our priest has a puzzled look. They both lean forward waiting for me to continue.

"They spoke to each other like old friends, but I couldn't hear their words. The encounter was brief and then Lycus continued his walk towards the Presbytere."

"Hmm, I can understand your suspicions. I know Lycus has some tendencies to the occult, but a connection with the loup garou is disconcerting. Those characters who kidnapped Etienne and put the demon in him may be beyond redemption."

"I think we should confront him." Grandmam shakes a finger in the air. "You claim a long acquaintance with the fellow."

"Yes, yes, I can agree, but remember that these creatures hide their evil natures well. It's possible that Lycus may have dealings with them without the knowledge of their evil character. I will contact him to get an answer."

I can't help thinking that we might be wiser to test him in some way without a confrontation. If he's in cahoots with them, then he's not our friend. And clearly not likely to admit a connection.

"Please wait, Father, and let me use my magic. I believe that I may have a plan to detect his loyalty to our cause. Give me two days. We have that until the moon confronts us. My concerns are all for Etienne, so I want to approach the question with great care."

Chapter Thirty-Six

Only one day we have before the full moon rises. I've followed Lycus Volcain for a day and night. In the morning he explored the market, questioned some vendors about their herbs and charms and purchased a goodly number. In the afternoon he returns to his living quarters on Rue Royal. It's a fine mansion. If he's the owner, there can be no doubt that his wealth must be considerable.

I spy on him through the windows in the courtyard. He has a male servant who prepares his mid-day meal. As the day continues, I watch him reading books that are stacked high on his desk. Later he takes out the bags of herbs and gris-gris he bought at the market then searches through another volume and takes notes in his journal. I almost fall asleep in the tree I've climbed to observe him.

At last when the sun slips behind the houses in our Quarter, he rises, puts his desk in order and leaves the room. It's my cue to climb down and watch to see if he'll be going out.

I wait on the banquette while the clouds turn red and orange, reflecting their colors in all the windows along the road. Darkness falls and all the colors fade. Ah, the front door swings open, and the Doctor steps out with his cape wrapped around his shoulders. I freeze against the building wall to see what his next move will be.

A carriage slows as it turns the nearby corner, but he doesn't signal it. Instead he strolls along Rue Royal as if he's out to catch a breath of the chilly night air. He continues past Rue St. Peter. I follow behind him, ducking into doorways, but managing to slink close by. His energy surprises me, and I have some difficulty keeping up with him. Now on Rue Bourbon he slows his pace at last.

He pauses at a gambling house and saloon. The city police have tried to outlaw these establishments of late, but they still exist although they have become discreet. When he knocks at the door, it opens on an entranceway that's painted brightly, and I can see fine carpets line the floors. As luck would have it two Creole gentlemen are leaving as Lycus steps in. I'm able to scoot behind the entrance door before I'm seen. The lighting's dim in these places which makes it easier for me to sneak behind the tables in the hallway.

Lycus speaks to one tall, well-dressed Creole man, who appears in charge of this establishment. I hear the doctor say, *a meeting*. The tall man nods and fortunately for me leads him to a private room that's right across the hall. I slip out from behind the buffet where I've been hiding and dart through the door behind them. It's magical that no one sees me. I think that my saints have blessed me with some shield this night.

Heavy drapes hang along one wall in this small room. The space is crowded with several tables and only one oil lamp in a corner. Another man is waiting at a table that sits in front of these dark purple drapes.

My fur bristles when I recognize, this fellow. Abel, the loup garou, beckons to the Doctor, pulling out a chair for him. I'm able to scramble quick behind a bookcase. The well-dressed Creole man walks to the door and calls a waiter. I crouch and wrap my tail around my hind legs. While I watch, the men request some wine.

They're alone after the waiter leaves the room. I edge closer to the table, so I can hear their words. My nose is almost poking out, but I know I'm still hidden behind these shelves. From my position I can watch them while I listen.

"At last we meet again." Abel smiles at Lycus.

I'm wondering to myself where his two companions might be. Of course, I suppose Yvette would not accompany him to a gambling house. Only cocottes would be around this establishment.

"Yes, I'm here at your request, Monsieur." Lycus removes his hat and places it on one side of the table.

For him to call Abel "Monsieur" seems strange to me, but then Dr. Lycus is partial to polite formalities. Still I notice Abel has raised an eyebrow, as if surprised. The door swings open and the waiter brings in a bottle of Claret with two goblets on a tray. He fills the glasses, accepts a tip from Abel, and leaves the room.

Abel raises his glass. "To you, our leader, master of the clan," he says. "I've wanted to speak to you for some time. You're the one that we want most to consult with."

Lycus frowns. "No, I do not claim to be your leader. When you contacted me, you offered some information, remedies and access to alkahest, a universal solvent so valuable for its medicinal qualities."

Abel puckers his lips. With a shrug of his shoulders, he leans forward. "But we explained that we need to gain the powers of the voudou queen to deliver this miraculous treatment. We believed that as the Master you would assist us in ultimately achieving the complete supremacy that's needed."

"Indeed, I was misled. I've learned quite a bit from working with the voudou queen you mention. I believe Lalin Bonheur inherited her healing powers. She's clearly gifted. Her talents work many benefits for her local clan. There's nothing of the negative that you implied."

"Ah, but she's just an uneducated girl. Gifted, yes, but we could do much greater things with the power she owns. You guaranteed that if we helped you travel to the city; you'd offer the expertise we needed."

Lycus pounds a fist against the table. The goblets wobble against the surface. "You're mistaken, Monsieur. There was no guarantee. You assume, because my family is noted for the curse for generations that I would promote your evil plan."

My fur bristles all around my body, as I watch Abel sneer at Lycus Volcain. He licks his lips then picks up his wine glass and takes a long drink before placing it down on the table.

"We would not have sponsored you. Many leads we gave you in your research. If you reject us, you can expect some repercussions "

Dr. Lycus rises from the table. The sudden move tips the surface and both glasses tip over. The wine spills across the surface, dripping to the floor, making rivers on the wooden planks.

"You dare to threaten me? It's you that can expect to have some problems." His voice grows louder, and he raises one open hand above Abel's head. I think he'll surely slap him and challenge him to a duel.

Abel stands abruptly. "Ha! Who will make us suffer? Your friend the priest? We'll take care of Etienne Legendre within a day now. Your connection with these holy, pious friends will not come to good for them. That's a promise!"

My little feline back is arched, and I feel a growl rising in my throat at the mention of my Etienne. Still I maintain my control and listen.

"Indeed, any harm that comes to Father Jules, Lalin Bonheur or Etienne Legendre through you and your followers, will be nothing compared to what I'll bring down on you. I'm not your leader, but I do have powers and the knowledge to deal with your kind. Never doubt it."

Lycus picks up his cape, plops his hat on in one brusque move and charges to the door. When it opens, I see my chance and streak across the room. Behind me I hear a shout.

"*Fils de putain!*" Abel yells these curses. I know he's seen me, but I am out the door too fast for him to catch me. I see Dr. Lycus striding down Rue Bourbon. His cape flies out behind him as he goes. In the opposite direction I scamper with all the speed that I can muster never turning around until I reach my house on Rue Burgundy.

Chapter Thirty-Seven

The full moon will rise tomorrow night. My love and I have arranged for him to be cloistered in the carriage house at our priest's home. Etienne intends to lead a normal day at the shipping office. He says he hopes to keep himself distracted with his work.

I've not yet told anyone of the experiences of the last evening. When I returned home, I was able to make my change and greet Etienne as usual. His work sometimes keeps him late. He also goes to see his parents on some evenings. With all the pressures he now feels, he wished to pay a visit to them before this next moon rise.

Both of us are full of worries and, although I cuddle with him through the late hours, neither of us sleep well this night. He holds me in his arms until the wee hours of the morning, but, when at last he drifts to sleep, my eyes remain wide open.

*　*　*

The moon shimmers like a gilded globe tonight. All preparations have been made. Grandmam and I have made our offerings to the saints. We locked Etienne in the room at the carriage house. He is, of course, despondent, but we try to comfort him with the plans for a ritual to rid him of the curse. Father Jules believes that it will be important to have a blood sample, and this makes the task quite difficult. How can this be obtained?

Grandmam Selene and I accompany Father to the cathedral. There our priest says Mass for Etienne's recovery, while we kneel and pray throughout the service.

Dr. Lycus has not appeared. He knows the full moon is upon us. He sent no word to our priest. I've remained silent about what I witnessed last night. Although I'm anxious to tell the story of Lycus and Abel and their meeting at the gambling house, it seems the wrong time to bring it up. Our concerns at this point are centered on my Etienne.

After Mass, as we're walking back to the Presbytere, we hear a scream like someone's being stabbed. The shrillness of the sound echoes off the walls of all the nearby houses.

Grandmam grabs my arm, and I see Father freeze in mid-step, but then we all break into a run. As we dash around the corner onto St. Ann, two creatures scramble across the road. On the banquette, a body's sprawled. Leaning up against a hitching post a woman clutches at her bloody shoulder.

When we reach the place where the body lies, I see that it's a man, a stranger to me. I kneel to see how I can help. Father Jules and Grandmam kneel with me. The victim groans. Father checks his pulse and my grandmam pulls out a bag of gris-gris to bring him back to consciousness. While they continue to give him some attention, I rise to see what I can do for the woman who stands nearby.

Her body shakes. She weeps as she tells me of the two monsters that just attacked them. "They were hairy like some wild animals and growling like angry bears. I thought surely they would rip us apart, but when you folks turned the corner, they dropped him on the banquette and ran." She touches her shoulder. "One shoved me as they jumped up. That's when he caught me here with his claw."

Indeed, her wound looks like a long scratch, but not too deep. I take her to a water trough and help her wipe away the blood with a piece of her torn sleeve. I turn again to assist Father with the man who's still lying flat across the banquette. His eyes are open, and he's describing the encounter that they've just experienced.

Grandmam stands up. She grabs my arm and leans close to my ear. "Lalin," she whispers, "I believe that Etienne's gone free from the carriage house. Go quickly to see what's happened."

"Yes, I fear the same," I say. I leave them there and run around the side of the building to check. In the brightness of the moonlight I see that the door to the room is open. It looks as if the hinges at the top might be broken. The padlock lies broken open on the courtyard stones. I take one fast look inside to see that my Etienne has escaped in his shifted form. There's also a small pool of blood on the floor. I'm in a state of shock. For several minutes I stand still, not knowing what to do next. Then I hear Grandmam's voice. She calls to me from the roadside along Rue St. Ann.

Filled with terror, I take in a long breath and tell myself that I must hold on to my control. "Erzulie," I pray in a low voice. "Give me the support I need to carry on. St. Michael, please, help us save my love this night, and let him not harm others." I close my eyes to wait for any guidance that might be offered.

Somehow, I know that Grandmam has something for me. I hear her calling once again. Back to the banquette, I run. Father Jules has managed to find a carriage to carry the man and woman to the Hospital of St. John to be treated there. He's talking to a gendarme, who carries a pistol in his belt. *Mon Dieu*, I know I must move faster than the wind to reach my love before he does some harm. My greatest fear is he'll be shot by the city police.

Grandmam meets me before I reach the others. She has something in her hand. "Take this, Lalin. If you can find Etienne, you must open the bag and throw all the salt on him. It's not our ordinary table salt. It's a unique mixture that I found in the ancient manuscripts that Father showed us. Etienne will lose his wolf form if you can get it on his body.

I say nothing. There's no question as to my next move. It occurs to me for one moment that I could shape shift myself. But it would only slow me down. With the bag of salt in my hands, I leave all of them behind.

The injured couple told us that the creatures ran across the road into the alleyway. I must find them. Dashing off with all the speed I can muster, my cloak flies open, and the fabric spreads like wings around me. I pray my magic gives me the swiftness I need. What I feel in my body is like a miracle! It's as if I'm flying. My feet touch the ground, but they barely skim the surface of the cobbles.

I'm through the alley in a moment. There's nothing and no one on the next road over. I dart around another corner. Pausing for a second, I listen for any sounds that might lead me in the right direction. So quiet, only a single cricket chirps from a nearby palm. I ask my saints which way to turn. A shadow in the moonlight gives me the answer. I'm not sure who or what it represents, but it's clearly in motion.

My feet fly, but even before I reach the next corner, I hear another scream. This one even louder than the other.

I rush to reach the next alley. At first, I see nothing, but a carriage gate swung wide open. The bag of salt I pull from my pocket as I run toward the gate.

Chapter Thirty-Eight

On first sight I can't tell them apart. The two hairy creatures hover over a man they've pinned against the wall. He appears to be a vagrant. Drunk and dirty he screams curses. The two loup garou haven't seen me yet. What an awful scene!

Then both shifters turn on me at once. Ah, I recognize Etienne by the clothing that remains on his back. His eyes are gleaming red just like his cohort, but he takes one step back. He does know it's me he faces. The other one makes a noisy growl and lunges towards me. At that moment, my wits come back to me, and I grasp the magical salt from the bag and throw a handful. It hits him on his snout then scatters on his shoulders. Falling backwards, he tumbles towards Etienne, and now I toss a larger handful onto Etienne.

Loud snarls and cries bounce off the walls while they stumble against each other and the vagrant man. The hobo yells again before falling to the cobble stones. I throw two more handfuls while the shifters stagger back against the wall. They throw their hairy arms up as if to block the spray of salt.

My Etienne is first to make the change. I watch, feeling full of fear but also fascination. The snout dissolves and his facial features gradually take shape. A human nose he has once again and manly lips instead of canine jaws. His claws begin to shrink, and fingers reappear. The hairiness that covers all his limbs melts into the ground beneath him, and his lovely skin looks fresh and normal once again. The transformation takes some minutes, but now he has his human body. All the clothing is in tatters, but my love, my Etienne, lies on the ground. His face smudged with dirt and streaks that may be blood.

Although my body trembles with the horror of the scene, my mind comes back to me. We have no time to waste. Abel slowly turns back into his man-self. I need to get Etienne away. There's no time to deal with this evil person. On my knees now, I strain to pull my love onto his feet. The hobo man has managed to creep away. He crawls behind the building while I watch.

Etienne looks so bedraggled, his shirt torn, and his jacket shredded. I try to brush off the dirt. "We must hurry, *mon cher*," I say to him.

He stares at me for one long moment, saying nothing. I pull him by the arm, and he does begin to follow me, but without a word. He's breathing heavy as we run together through the alleys to reach the Presbytere.

At the next corner when I turn around, he' s half a block behind me. He leans against a building wall. I rush to check on him. He begins to cough; I fear he'll choke with all the noise he's making.

"We've not far to go now," I say. "If you need help, you can lean against me, and we'll move together."

He gasps and sinks to the cobbles of the alley. My tall and handsome man lies flat against the stones. What can I do? I think hard to myself. There's no way I can lift him from the ground.

"St. Michael, help us!" I grasp my amulet as I pray to him. "Give us your strength!"

We've three more city blocks to travel before Rue St. Ann. I know I can't leave Etienne here alone. His eyes are closed, but his lips move in silence. I pray again for any guidance the saints can give. While I whisper prayers, the sound of footsteps echoes in the night. Someone's running through the alleys behind us. Likely it's Abel coming after us. He'll try to get Etienne away from me. This I know for certain.

Up I jump. I can think of nothing but to run back to the next corner where I stopped last. Once there I see a figure in the dim light. Yes, someone comes down the banquette. It can't be Abel. There's no way he could get that far ahead of us.

"Help," I call out. "Help us please!"

The person begins to run towards me. Then I see the black cape swirling out behind him and recognize Dr. Lycus Volcain. Within a few seconds he reaches me.

"Lalin," he says, "I just came from the Presbytere. We've been searching for you. I heard Etienne broke out. What happened?"

His eyes blink rapidly. He speaks in such a raspy voice. I wonder if I'm right to trust him. But with the prayers to the saints, I can only hope he may be here to help.

"Etienne's back there. Come quickly." I beckon to him and rush to the alley with him behind me.

When I see what's ahead, I cry out. My worst fears face me head on. Abel stands right in front of my Etienne. In an instant he bends, grasping my love by the shoulders. "Let me help you, my brother," I hear him say and then he turns to me. "I'll take care of him now." He nods his head in my direction.

Then Dr. Lycus steps into the alley. The two men freeze in place for one moment. Lycus breaks the silence as he strides forward.

"Release the man! You've caused enough grief and pain to these people and who knows how many more before them."

Abel steps back from Etienne, facing Lycus with an angry scowl. "You're one of us, Lycus Volcain! Call off the charade. Tell Lalin Bonheur the truth."

Behind him Etienne begins to shake his head. His strength comes back to him. Slowly he rises, getting steady on his feet.

Dr. Lycus takes a firm step forward. "Indeed, I'm suffering from a family curse. But you're wrong to say I'm one like you. I seek a cure for myself and *ma famille*. We renounce the evil powers that your kind are noted for."

Abel turns to me with a smirk, and shrugs his shoulders, gesturing to Lycus with one hand. "Surely you know that he seeks to destroy you. We know him, Yvette, and me. He came to help us, but seems he's decided to help himself to your power instead. A traitor clearly. No one to trust."

My body quakes with fear and doubt. I pray St. Michael will give me guidance. Abel, I know, projects only an evil aura. With Lycus I feel unsure.

Etienne comes to me at this point and with some relief I fall into his arms. He holds me close, whispering in my ear. "My Lalin, I haven't lost all my control. I can defend us both."

Lycus stands in steely silence, as if waiting for someone to address him. Etienne turns suddenly as though on instinct. The doctor has pulled a small pistol from his vest. He aims straight for Abel, but he's caught by the other man's fist. Still Lycus remains on his feet, lunging once again at the younger man. But this time he drops the pistol. The two men struggle. Dr. Lycus tries to maintain his balance. He manages to kick the weapon towards Etienne. At that moment Abel strikes Lycus on the chin and knocks him against the wall. The loup garou man draws a silver dagger from his belt.

My love reacts and dives quickly to retrieve the pistol which lies between him and the two men struggling against the wall. He has it in his hands and rises to confront them. "Step back!" he yells.

Lycus regains his control. "Trust me," he shouts. "I mean no harm to either of you. I've learned this man's my enemy as much as he is yours."

I pray hard and hold on to my love. He aims the pistol now. The shot cracks through the silence of the night.

Chapter Thirty-Nine

The bullet hits Abel's shoulder. He howls like the monster he really is. Grasping at his shoulder, he stares at the blood dripping through his fingers. Etienne aims the pistol at his chest. Dr. Lycus stands unmoving to the side.

Yelling curses at the night air, Abel backs away from us. As he staggers down the alley, a shadow falls across the moonlit cobblestones. Growing larger, a phantom shade descends from above. Giant wings stir the air. This creature hovers over Abel. Has it been waiting, watching from the night sky? It drops lower; its talons, extending from its feathered body, hook around his torso. Wings spread, feathers quiver as it rises. Black eyes fall on me. A pain jabs me in my chest, as if those eyes have a wounding power. In an instant I grab my amulet, hold it up above my head and whisper prayers to St. Michael and Erzulie, our Blessed Mother.

The bird squawks loudly against my holy emblem. Abel makes a clumsy climb onto its back. Up they soar, much higher than our heads. Wings flutter, sending gusts of air around us. To the rooftops they go. I hold on to Etienne as tightly as I can. He wraps one arm around me. I feel the strength reviving in his muscles. It's clear he's becoming more himself again.

A few dark feathers drift down. Dr. Lycus watches with us, as Abel and his partner sail above the building, disappearing over rooftops and behind the chimneys. Lycus picks up his cloak that fell on the stones in the scuffle and turns to us again.

"Fiends," he says, "and that's not the last we'll see of them. The woman brings evil more than the men. She has a pretty face, but her heart's filled with darkness. They'll not give up so easy."

Etienne faces him. The tension in his voice makes waves in the air. "What more do you know of them?" he asks.

Lycus stares at him in silence, then speaks in a rough whisper. "They heard about me from my followers. I too bear the curse. In truth I came to the city at first to meet them." He clasps his hands and hugs them tight against his chest. "They claimed they had access to many cures and remedies. All lies."

I still feel doubts about this man, as I listen to him explain his connections. But then a glow begins to circulate around him. Yes, I recognize this sign my saints have sent. At last they send a stronger signal. "Then you swear to us your practice is for the good? We have nothing to fear from you?" I ask. Etienne takes my hand and speaks to him again."Lalin's been frightened of you since our first meetings."

He nods. I wonder if he can see the glow. "I hope you can believe me," he says. "I have some unique abilities. It's true, but I bring no threat to either of you. I only wished to learn something of Lalin's talents. Surely Father Jules has vouched for me. The priest and I've been friends since our boyhood in France." Lycus extends his hand to my Etienne.

* * *

The three of us walk together to the Presbytere. We look for Father Jules and Grandmam. We ask the servant girl, Georgette, who stands on the banquette, holding out a lantern. She tells us that they set out to find me after I ran away. I know my grandmam can't go too fast. They haven't gotten far.

"Shall we look for them?" I say.

"Leave that to me," Lycus volunteers. "Etienne needs time to recover, and you should stay with him."

He hurries off in the opposite direction from where we came. Etienne and I go inside the building. I must have a look at the scratches on his arms. They will need cleaning. Father's maid brings us a basin full of water, some soap, and towels. I set about to help him with these minor wounds.

It's almost dawn. Sunlight filters through the drapes in this parlor. I feel relief that the full moon has faded in the daylight. I had worries that I might need to use the salt a second time. I'm grateful to Grandmam Selene for her knowledge. She's the real Queen and without her I wouldn't have the knowledge. I only follow the magic I've learned from her.

Not long now before we hear footsteps on the front stoop. The door swings open and Father, Grandmam Selene and Dr. Lycus all appear. Grandmam rushes to us without a word. She hugs us both.

"*Merci, Bondye*," she says, raising her hands to the heavens. "My old heart was near to giving out with the fears I had."

I smile at her. "It's true we must give thanks before the morning's gone."

Father Jules comes close to Etienne. "How are you, my son?" he asks. "You need some time to recover that's for certain. There's not much time to waste. We must begin to plan for the exorcism."

"Has Lycus told you how I found Etienne and all the story about Abel?" I ask.

The answer comes from the doctor. "They were headed back this way when I saw them. I've told them what I saw."

Etienne and I are seated at a small tea table where we've cleansed his scrapes. Father pulls up more chairs, calling to Georgette to bring out some brandy. Soon she brings the decanter from a cabinet.

"I think we all need a strong drink," he states. With the snifters filled, Father passes them around.

Etienne gulps his down as does Dr. Lycus. Grandmam and I take a sip and place our glasses on the table.

"What a ghastly night! I feel as though I lost my mind for some long hours." Etienne points to the bottle and lets our priest fill his glass again. "I can't explain it. Something like the last full moon when I was locked up, but this time I have more memories." He takes a sip of brandy. "How I got free, I don't remember. But the sight of the loup-garou, Abel, is clear to me. Someone else is with us. Not sure who."

"Was it, Yvette?" I feel the tension even as I ask the question. And I tell myself to stay calm.

Etienne rubs his forehead with both hands. "It could've been."

I turn to Lycus. "What is their connection? You must know. Are these shapeshifters all related? Blood relatives?"

"You must believe. I swear I don't know them well. But in the dealings, I've had with them, it came clear. They're all close cousins. The three stay in a fine house that's owned by their aunt."

"Madame Nanette," I say and nod at Etienne. Then I give Lycus a long hard stare. "Do you know the woman?"

"Again, I've told you most all I know. They learned of me from my own distant relatives who have a plantation near the river. They found out about the family curse and cajoled my kin to contact me. Then through letters and some more mystic ways, they made their first connections." The glow has followed him, and I feel comfort that my saints have given me a sign.

Etienne empties his glass of brandy and places it on the table. "Enough for this night," he says. "We all need rest." He rises and, facing our priest, claps his hands together and breaths out a puff of air. "Father, I will meet with you tomorrow to discuss what we need to do to prepare for the remedy you recommend. Lalin will be by my side. If an exorcism is needed, then so be it."

Chapter Forty

It's Sunday, so Etienne and I have the day to sleep, if we wish. However, with the events of the past night, the tensions are too high for much real rest. I lie in bed with edgy apprehension. After getting Grandmam to her house and bidding goodbye, we headed straight to my small home on Rue Burgundy.

My love tosses in his restless sleep. Time, I need, to think things through. Quietly I slip out of bed. In my kitchen room I brew a cup of café, then sit on my courtyard bench, staring up as the skies grow brighter.

I decide, it's time for me to write a note to Etienne. Leaving the coffee and the milk on the stove to heat up later, I tiptoe into my boudoir to find some clothes to dress for the day. With my hair wrapped in my tignon, I take my lightest cape, drape it on my shoulders, and silently creep out my front door, locking it behind me. It's to our cathedral I go now.

The first Mass has ended when I arrive. Father Jules speaks with a few of his parishioners in the narthex. I kneel at a candle altar and pray a rosary while I wait.

My priest comes to me when his parishioners leave. He knows I've come to seek him out so early to ask questions. He takes me to a small bench in an alcove. There he left a stack of books. We both sit. He takes my hand to hold for just a minute and smiles at me.

"I see all your worries in your face," he says.

"I have many things to ask, Father."

When I express my doubts about his friend, Lycus Volcain, he assures me once again that he does trust the man. He explains that in the early years of their friendship he learned that Lycus claimed a family curse that haunted him. Details were always left unsaid.

Stories circulated that his grandpapa was accused of a murder in their home village. The grandpa disappeared. Some days later local men, chopping wood in the forest were attacked by a wild animal. The strange creature resembled a wolf, they said. One man used his ax to kill the thing. When they brought sentries from a nearby town, the creature's body was gone. Instead the body of the Duke of Languedoc lay on the ground. The duke was his grandpapa and the leader of the Volcain clan.

"All these tales came secondhand to me, not through Lycus. I don't know the truth even though I tried to learn more. Few people would talk about the crime and the strange findings." Father Jules sighs and frowns but continues. "In the early days, Lycus and I attended Mass together. But he lost his faith and we drifted apart. For some years there was little contact. He wrote letters from time to time."

"Did you know that he later studied medicine?" I ask.

"Yes, he sent a letter when he finished with his training."

I'm surprised when Father begins to tell me of the work he did in foreign missions. This morning he reveals much more about his experience, and how his friend, Lycus, had an interest in the customs and healing methods in those remote areas. The old remedies offered many cures. And he also felt it was there he'd find an answer for the curse that troubled him. Father believed the curse was an illusion of some kind. Although the legend of the loup garou was a part of local lore in the countryside. He never took it seriously.

"I suppose at that young age I didn't recognize the fears that haunted my friend and his family. It wasn't until Lycus turned up at my door last year that I began to understand."

As the weeks passed, he tells me that they frequently met for a meal or glass of anisette in the evening. He recognized the man was troubled, but still had no idea of the difficulties that he faced.

"I was truly delighted to see him." He smiles, as he continues. " I never believed the legends of the shape-shifters. Fantastic tales, I thought. Nothing to take seriously."

"Did you ask him questions about his troubles?" I ask.

"No, but I began to listen when he shared the information he'd stumbled on in his search for answers. About that time all the rumors about the shifters started in New Orleans. Injuries and deaths. Many of the faithful here were affected. But the idea of wolf men roaming through our city seemed absurd. Still the evidence grew and grew. And then I learned more about you and your grandmam. I've finally had to accept the truth of mystic powers that I never believed before."

"You remember when you saw my gift to shift into my feline form. Through my saints I'm able to pass the gift to Etienne."

"Yes, I had to face my disbelief. Life carries more mysteries than the church has taught me." Father shakes his head. I know his faith is strong, but he struggles to mix the doctrine with the realm of magic.

"For me, the mystic powers are all the same. What the church taught me does not conflict with my magic." I hold up my amulet of St. Michael for him to see.

"I know you bring many blessings to your people, Lalin. But my training brands your rituals as evil and demonic." He claps his hands together and his lips tighten in a frown. "Still I've learned to accept that they bring good things. Your healing work produces miracles." And now his face relaxes while he nods.

I sigh. It's time for me to ask. "Father, are we ready for Etienne's cure, the exorcism?"

He hesitates before he speaks. "I performed one some years ago here in the city. With Etienne we also need to use the blood collected. The ritual will, of course, be in Latin. It's important to be exact. There are several old texts that I have to reread to make sure."

"Will Dr. Lycus be present or involved?" I ask.

"Lycus has offered to bring wolfsbane." Father taps a finger against his forehead, as if trying to remember something. "I think the herb isn't needed but can do no real harm."

"So, you think his presence isn't necessary?"

"I do think we should have him here." He clears his throat, pressing his lips together then continues. "It's possible," he says, hesitating once again, "that we may need him to restrain the subject. It will be a very tense and trying time for all of us."

I nod, but inside my head I have some frightening thoughts. None of us know what the outcome might be. Grandmam and I, with all our knowledge, have never had to rid someone of such a curse. I hadn't thought a demon could possess him in such a way. I do believe we need our priest to save us from this evil thing.

Father reaches for his stack of books. "You know it's also true that Lycus wants to rid his family of the curse."

"Yes, I hear what you say, but how does it affect him? Does he shift to the wolf shape too? I'm confused about his problem."

"He seems to have control over himself. High doses of wolfsbane he claims. It's someone else that he's most concerned about. You see he has a son left back in France."

Chapter Forty-One

It's nearing mid-day by the time I reach home again. Etienne should be out of bed by now. He needed extra rest after last night, but I've never known him to sleep till noon.

"Mon cher," I call as I walk through the house. No answer. The boudoir door is open. "Etienne, where are you?"

The bed has been made, although not so neat. Pillows lie on the center of the counterpane. I smile. He did at least make some effort to leave things tidy. As I walk closer to the bed, I see a note left on the bedside table.

Dear Lalin,

What a terrible night we had. Where have you gone so early? Found coffee on the stove and rolls, but not my love nearby. You must be off to Mass to pray, so I will leave too. I need to see my parents. I know they're sick with worry. Father Jules may ask for me, but I must have some time to think things through. You stay safe. I will see you late this evening.

Etienne

It's time for me to make offerings to the saints to thank them for helping us get through the awful night. While I'm thinking that I might go to Grandmam Selene to make the altar, I straighten up the linens on the bed. The pillows lie askew, so I pick them up to smooth the covers.

"*Que diable!*" I say out loud. Many gray splotches pepper the counterpane. Bending to look closer, I see they're feathers. When I pick one up, it quivers in my palm. The color's a bluish grey. It does remind me of the shape-shifting Yvette, but as I stand there thinking of this awful image, a sound breaks my concentration. Hurrying to find what brings this noise, I see the door to the courtyard swinging on its hinges. It makes a whining sound in the breeze.

I wonder why this door's left open, and, when I go to close it, I find that there's a blue grey cluster near the door. If the door was left ajar, perhaps it could be just a bird that flew in. The courtyard door I keep locked, if I go out, but Etienne was here. Perhaps he forgot to lock it after going to the kitchen room. I sigh and shake my head. I don't want more suspicions. I believe in more important mysteries to solve at this point.

✷ ✷ ✷

It's early evening when I walk home from Grandmam Selene's. The scents of spring drift in the air. Wisteria flaunts its purple blooms. These vines climb along the walls in our Quarter. Fragrant blossoms hang in purple clusters like giant ornaments to decorate the iron gates along the banquette. At least we have the season's colors to give us cheer in these hard times.

Grandmam and I spent the afternoon in prayer and study. Father loaned us books that contain chants and summons said to banish demons. Although some mambos may perform their own rituals to rid folks of these evil spirits, we believe the ceremony will be best performed by the holy man, our priest.

When I reach my house on Rue Burgundy, I find that Etienne has come back from his parents' house. He greets me with a warm embrace.

"How are you, my love?" he asks. When he gives me a sweet kiss, I catch the scent of anisette on his breath. His smile tells me he's had a pleasant visit with his parents.

"You look relaxed," I say. "I trust your mama and papa are feeling well."

"Hmm, I have to say, since they know nothing of the misery that we've just suffered, it's like an escape from everything." He closes his eyes for a moment. "Perhaps I should tell them something in case things don't go well with the plan."

I appreciate his concern for his family, but they always keep their distance from me. His papa has been kind to me in many ways. It's true too that it was through Monsieur Legendre that I met Etienne. The money for the *plaçage* came from him, and that's the money that pays all my expenses. However, Etienne's mama has never recognized or contacted me in anyway. Still I must always keep respect for them for my lover's sake.

"You know best, *mon cher*. But I do understand that you don't like to worry them with the difficulties and stresses that we face." I kiss him lightly on his ear. "I had a long talk with Father Jules this morning. He's preparing for the ritual. Do you have a time to meet with him?"

"Yes, I have to make arrangements. Today I couldn't face it. I needed time to rest and think. What did you learn from him this morning?"

"Well, he explained that the words are all in Latin, but, of course, that's not surprising. Some volumes, he showed me, that described the ritual." I shrug my shoulders. "I told him that we would come together for him to give us more detail."

"We'll go tomorrow evening then," he says.

"Yes, that will be good." Dr. Lycus runs through my head now, and I decide to see what Etienne thinks about him. "I questioned Father about our friend, Lycus. He takes a positive view of him. Says that they have been friends for many, many years, and, even though the man has a strangeness about him, he trusts him. Do you agree?"

A puzzled look flashes on his face. He squints and rubs his nose. "I can't explain it, but I confess I feel some connection with him. He helped to save me in the alley, as I remember. He had a scuffle with Abel, am I right? We didn't talk about it but ..."

"Right, we haven't talked about it. Dr. Lycus had a pistol. Without that weapon we might have lost the struggle in the alley." Both Etienne and I are silent for several minutes. I wait for his response.

"The details escape me, and I recall Lycus being there. I know there was a struggle, but the gun I don't remember."

"It's true. We've had no time to talk till now."

My mind takes a distracted turn. It's feathers, I'm thinking of again. Yes, feathers. I wonder, does he recall the giant bird in the alley? I must ask. "Etienne, do you remember the bird that came to carry Abel away?"

He nibbles at his lower lip and shakes his head. "No, what happened then? I have no memory of it."

"It had to be Yvette. We know she shifts into a bird-thing. Something like a hawk, but much larger. I thought another time, a bat. But, no, it has feathers."

"Yes, a bird like the one that attacked us on Rue St. Ann that day on our way to the Presbytere. What an awful memory!" He stares at me for several seconds. "Are we sure it's her?"

I watch his face. He can't lie to me. This I know. For some reason he's blacked out the final scene from the alley. What troubles me now is my memory of the gray-blue feathers on the counterpane. Yes, and by the courtyard door too. I'm wondering what I should ask. If it comes up again, I'll feel all the worse. It's important that I stay alert to anything that might bring problems to us.

"Etienne, when I came back from the visit with Father Jules, I found something odd here."

He jerks his head around. Eyebrows raised. "What? Something wrong in the house?"

"Nothing serious, I hope, but by chance did you see some feathers in the boudoir or by the courtyard door? I thought a blue jay or even a small blue heron had flown in." The image of the giant bird in the alley flutters through my head, and I try to hold back signs of the tension that well up in my throat.

He tilts his head, as if he's trying to recall something. "I saw nothing, Lalin. Wasn't that door locked this morning?"

"Yes, I left it locked, but when I returned the door was open and a little pile of feathers lay scattered on the floor."

CHAPTER FORTY-TWO

Etienne had a goodnight's sleep last night. I'm happy for that, but the mystery of the feathers puzzles me. We both checked the door and two windows to make sure that nothing was left open.

His priority is to contact our priest to set a time for an evening meeting. I hope Father has time today. Since I read so little Latin, the books that he loaned us are not much help. My love knows more than me, but not enough to understand the fine points of this important ritual.

When I'm alone again, I take the time to run things through my mind. Once again it occurs to me that I need to keep an eye out for the loup garou. I have this morning free to take my feline shape and search the Quarter for Abel. Most likely he's healing from his wound. That injury would not be too serious unless there's infection. He may even be out of the house today.

* * *

Gray clouds hover over all our roads and buildings, while I pad my way along Rue Toulouse. The air feels wet. My black fur glistens in the dampness. People walking on the banquette glance up at the sky, and remark to one another that it surely looks like rain. I'm on my way to Rue Royal to check at the house of the loup garou and Yvette.

A light rain begins to fall. Even with my thick fur, a slight shower gives me a chill. I scamper between the doorways, stopping under stoops to shake myself. Some folks hurry along with umbrellas held above their heads. I follow close behind them. A few more minutes it will take me to reach the house on Royal. From the banquette there's no way to tell if anyone's at home, so I will have to find the windows.

I slink low to squeeze under the wrought iron carriage gate. Once in the courtyard, I gaze up at the second floor. Strangely, no balconies or galleries inside this courtyard, but if I climb up the one big palm tree, I can at least peek in the windows. Up I go, claws digging in hard. The rain has made the palm trunk slick, but I manage to cling and clamber to the window level. The boudoir on the second floor is a spacious one, and from the tree top I have a good view into one large window. No one's in the room, and I am disappointed after all my climbing effort. But the window is cracked open the bedroom door's ajar. Have patience, I tell myself. Resting on a broad palm limb, I tuck my front paws under, wrap my tail around me and wait.

The rain subsides. I try not to fall asleep. An hour passes or maybe two before a sound alerts me. A woman's voice, yes, Yvette comes through the door into the boudoir.

"I'll take my chances." She's talking to someone outside the room. My feline ears can hear quite well even at a distance.

She claps her hands together, turns towards the door, and calls out. "I know how to charm him. I bewitch him." With a giggle, she continues. "Don't worry. He won't remember."

The bedroom door swings wide open, and Abel, the loup garou man, strides in. "Yvette, you'll never win him. The man must certainly despise you at this point."

She swirls around to face him. Anger makes her voice shrill. "What a lie that is! We would be married now if she hadn't found out. We were engaged. Arrangements had been made."

"I'm warning you. Give up this plan! Whatever it is you think you can do, won't work. We have one purpose here and that's to take the power from this mambo Queen. There's no place for your obsession."

What's this? The woman's mad! Her evil never ends. And the loup garou man always plots to steal the power. My tiny heart jumps like a cricket in my chest.

While I listen to them argue, lightning flashes in the clouds, and thunder roars through the air. A heavy shower bursts from the grey skies above me. Shivering, I crawl between two palm fronds still watching. Inside the room, Abel rushes to the bedroom window and slams it closed. There's no chance for me to hear now.

From the tree I still watch. Yvette shakes a finger at her cousin. He stalks toward the door. Even though I hear no words now, I have much concern about the doings of this evil woman.

✳ ✳ ✳

I'm drenched when I get back to my home. There's no way for me to keep my cat-self dry, and I didn't want to spend all day hiding in the palm tree. Although I shift back to be myself, I still feel cold and damp. I take the time to heat some water for a bath. With warm water in my tub, I enjoy a relaxing soak and think about what I have heard at the house on Rue Royal.

I lay back against the copper edge with a small pillow to rest my head against. A long, deep breath helps me relax and close my eyes. Inside my head the scene comes back to me. What's she describing? Is this something she remembers from the past with my Etienne? *We were engaged... we would be married now ...* It sounds like she's recalling last year, when she used her magic to put some spell on him in Natchez. *He won't remember.* Somehow, it's these words that worry me.

Lying there in the warm water, I pray for some intervention from my saints. What about the dark blue feathers on the bed? Could she have been inside my house? Inside my boudoir? It comes to me that I must make offerings to Erzulie and St. Michael. With their help I'll get some answers.

After I have dried myself and put the tub away, I dress in clean clothes and begin to set up the altar for the saints. Blue and white candles I take out and some lacy altar doilies that will please Erzulie. Inside my armoire I find the box that has my best rosary and a beautiful picture of her with golden hair nearly covered in a pale blue veil. Along with these things I bring out some rum and sweet cakes, fruit, and perfume. All I place on the altar that I make.

On my knees, I pray, but then Erzulie calls me to dance for her. When I stand, I feel her presence. She's here with me. Rising on my toes, I pirouette around the room. My feet move slow at first. My body sways. My spine loosens as I bend forward and then lean back almost to the floor. A translucent mist enfolds the room. Erzulie takes control, and I struggle to keep some power so I can find out what I need to know

I keep the movement going while she fills my head with pictures. Her beauty floats around me first; then she moves through me. Her presence brings a fragrance to the room. Roses, yes, a lovely scent fills my nose. My Erzulie is always bursting with sweetness and yet so sensual, she is.

Ah, my knees grow weak. One last spin I make before I go down slowly to the floor. "Please let me see." I call out to her. When I close my eyes, the scene grows up around me. What appears I can't believe. All the sweetness melts and leaves a sour scent. My worst fears rise to haunt me. It's like the snake sinks its fangs into my heart.

CHAPTER FORTY-THREE

It takes me time to recover from what Erzulie let me see. Pain travels through my body. The feathers did indeed mean the worse that I could imagine. First, I'm angry, then very sad, but as I think hard, I realize what I must do.

The words *he won't remember* echo in my ears. Etienne doesn't know, of that I feel completely sure. The creature fluttered through my courtyard door. Winging through the parlor into my boudoir, it hung above our bed where Etienne slept so soundly. I held my breath and watched the thing descend to the counterpane.

This giant bird shakes itself, scattering feathers, as it settles in the center of our counterpane. It pauses there, folding wings close against its body. Black eyes blinking, this bird gazes at my Etienne. But then the nightmare grows even worse. A transformation.

No, I can't say that I'm surprised at the shifting of this creature's shape. But still the scream I hear comes from my throat. How could this happen? I cry for my saints to stop it. There's no way for me to intervene.

Turning on our bed, sliding closer to my Etienne, the naked woman slips her body beneath the counterpane and between the sheets. Her creamy skin, her plumpness now wrapped around my love and nothing I can do to stop this scene.

I come through a haze from the horror of this nightmare. My body shaking hard against the floor. Like a crazy woman, I thrash about. How long I lay there, I couldn't say. When I come totally awake from the dreadful dream, my hands and arms are sore and bruised. Never have I shed so many tears.

"Take deep breaths," I tell myself. With all the pain I feel, I say some prayers to my St. Michael and hold his amulet against my heart. Erzulie let me see the awful truth. It's hard to be thankful for the misery I feel, but still I light more candles to please her. "Please help me destroy this wickedness," I whisper, as I prepare to see my love when he returns to me.

* * *

Etienne has met with Father Jules. He brings home more treatises about the ritual that must be performed. He tells me that tomorrow evening we need to go to the Presbytere to make the final preparations with our priest. I will ask Grandmam Selene to come with us too. She must learn as much as possible about the exorcism. I will need her there with me on that night.

Father has told Etienne that he intends to ask Dr. Lycus to attend for support. I may also contact Apolline. It would be a comfort to have a friend nearby.

Etienne and I have our supper in my small dining room. Never would I mention what I saw in the vision. He can't be blamed for this abomination. I had time to think what I will do. My plan develops with discretion. He'll not be alone in the house of that you can be sure. It will be difficult to follow him throughout his day, but, if it comes to that, I must find some way to keep her from him. Watchful, watchful, I must be.

We talk tonight about our fears of the curse and the cure. He sips a glass of wine on the sofa in my parlor. Although I try my best to blot out the scene Erzulie sent me, it runs through my mind like bad memories tend to do.

"I'll make sure all the doors and windows are locked," I say. "It's certain that some bird flew in this morning and left its feathers." I swallow hard, breathe deep to keep my voice calm.

He smiles and slides up close to me on the sofa, kissing me softly on the cheek. "Are you fearful of a bird, my love?" he asks.

I look into his eyes for any signs, but see nothing, but their brightness. If he only knew, the level of my concern. "Perhaps I am," I say. "But you saw nothing. No bird, no feathers..."

His laughter startles me. "Lalin, I know we have things to fear, but a bird seems to be so small a threat at this point. What is it that worries you so much?"

Wishing I could look into his mind, I shake my head. "You may be right. The bird could be harmless like a normal creature should be. But experiences with the loup garou and giant flying creatures have made me watchful. Evil shifters bring dangers."

* * *

Etienne and I meet with Father Jules, and he gives us all the details of the ritual he'll perform. He explains how he'll use the blood collected from my love. I am surprised when he shows us a vial that he saved from the puddle left on the floor when he escaped that night from the carriage house. We must have his blood from the loup garou form. I had forgotten this. Our priest is clever to have the foresight and remember that the sample must be ready for the ceremony.

Father will contact Dr. Lycus to make sure that he knows all the plans for the exorcism which will be performed within a week. It must take place before the next full moon. For my part I pay a visit to Grandmam Selene to give her all the information we have learned.

It's been a tiring day for him and worse than that for me. Etienne worked all day at the shipping office, while I spent my time preparing herbal treatments for my followers. Although I'm preoccupied with fears about the next moves of this monster bird, I force myself to erase any thoughts of jealousy or anger. My central purpose will be to protect my Etienne. I pray for the strength for my intention.

We relax together this night, cuddling on my sofa. When he kisses me and holds me with a strong embrace, I whisper in his ear that I want him now this instant. So quick he scoops me up in his arms and carries me off to the boudoir. Our bodies tangle in our passion; arms, legs, all parts of us become entwined. The love on this night is so intense that we're both exhausted from the ardor that we share.

* * *

It's my intent to wake early this morning. If I am right, the bird thing, Yvette, will return as soon as Etienne's alone. First, I make coffee in the kitchen room. I write a note to tell my love I'm leaving for the market, then I dress, lock the doors and leave one window open to let in the fresh air. I kiss Etienne lightly on the cheek, so not to rouse him and leave the house.

When I reach the corner of Burgundy and Toulouse, I duck into a nearby alleyway. To my saints I say the words I need to make my change. Within some few minutes I have four paws, soft black fur and just a touch of white to make the perfect color change. In the feline form, I pad down the alley. Climb one wooden wall that circles a neighbor's garden. From there I scamper across that courtyard to reach another wall which leads me back to my own house. As it happens, I arrive in time to crawl through the open window and hide behind the armoire in my boudoir. Here I'll wait. I do believe the evil comes.

Etienne turns in our bed, but I can see his eyes are closed. He's sleeping with a little snore. I only have to wait perhaps half an hour before I hear the flutter outside the window. Mon Dieu, my worst fears lurk in the courtyard. It's true. Now the large bird slips through the open window. It sails around the bed, circling, descending at times as if to take a closer look at my lover.

I feel my small heart skip a beat and can't restrain a tiny hiss. Out I step on my soft paws, slinking to the bed. My belly slides against the floor. The bird doesn't see me, as I creep towards the center of the room, pausing near the canopy bed. She makes one more loop. Swooping down, she lights near the center of the counterpane. No time to spare, I say to myself. My move must come before she starts to make her change.

Crouching low on my haunches as I prepare to spring, I hear my lover's voice. He gasps or groans. I'm not sure which. With that, I push off. A flying pounce, I make, in time to see that Etienne lies half awake.

She's changing now, so quickly. I jump on her even as her body grows into its woman form. Feathers fly in all directions. Shrieks and squawks fill the air with her anger. My claws dig deep, but already her change has come. The Yvette squirms over to her side and rises on her knees. With one hand she grabs me by the neck and slams me against the bedstead. Etienne remains frozen in those minutes, his eyes so wide, his face contorted. It's then my saints perform a miracle for me. My body shifts to my human form.

Still her hands clutch my neck and bang my head against the wooden bed frame. Thankfully, I have strong legs. Kicking hard against her torso, I throw her off me. Her back's against the mattress now at one end of the bed. She grabs a handful of my hair, pulling hard, but I bring one knee down hard onto her chest.

Etienne's up off the bed, staring at us. "Get your pistol!" I yell at him.

Chapter Forty-Four

My love stands in the center of the room with the pistol gripped tightly in his hands. I slide away from this woman. Her eyes are closed. But then she screams so loud, I get a sharp pain in my ears. Rising off the bed, she faces Etienne, and I think for one moment that she will attack him even with the pistol pointing at her.

"You must still love me," she shouts. "We planned to marry."

He shakes his head and looks from her to me. "Yvette, I don't remember anything of that."

I want to cry out for him to shoot her. How can he stand there talking to her?

She moves closer to him. The pistol still aimed straight at her chest. "Etienne, it's me you love not her." She reaches for him, and I am horrified to see him lower the pistol to his side. Now she wraps her arms around his shoulders, pushing her plump breasts against his chest and plants her lips against his mouth.

By St. Michael and all my saints, I fly at her, grab her by the shoulders and pull her off him. She wrestles with me, but I use all my strength to pin her arms behind her back. I see Etienne blinking, as if dust's blowing in his eyes. He shudders, stepping backwards. Ah, she's putting spells on him. The pistol drops to the floor.

She wriggles free and scrambles to retrieve the gun. I'm too quick for her this time. I grab the butt with both hands. When she tries to pull it from me, the pistol fires. Yvette falls back, and I see she took the bullet in her arm.

She screams again, dropping to the floor. "I'll kill you for this!"

Etienne and I watch unmoving, while she thrashes on the boudoir carpet for several seconds, mumbling words I can't make out. Her body begins to change. Shrinking first, then her arms sprout feathers. Wings spread, legs spindle thin and talons burst through the skin. With the transformation complete, she skitters low along the floor. Her wound leaves a bloody trail, as she spreads her wings. She lifts into the air, struggling to fly even with her injured wing.

I see a broomstick propped against the wall, and move to grab it, thinking I can swat her down. Before I have it in my hands, she's regained some strength. She soars above me even as I aim for her and then sails through the door. I run right behind her. She's reached the window, flaps through the opening and out into the courtyard. Blood still dripping from her injured wing. She drops low, and I think that she'll surely fall. But then, lifted by the breeze, she rises. Above the rooftops, she flutters and finally disappears.

✳ ✳ ✳

It could be the worst day of my life. This one's left me with shakes and fears I've never felt. Many worries I've had for Etienne, but when this predatory woman appears, I know I must fight for him. She was able to put him in a trance before. His defenses break down with the hex she plants on him. It appears the spell may be broken. She lost the battle in this attack.

My love and I sit on the bed for how long a time I'm not sure. The morning sunlight spills across the room. I hear him mumbling in the silence. He stands up, walks to the center of the room, and turns to face me.

"Lalin, *mon amour*, I feel as though I've been beaten up. My ears are ringing. It's like I lost my consciousness. What happened? Did I have a spell?"

I stare at him. Has he no memory of what happened? "We were attacked by the evil bird, the shifter. You don't remember?" I want to shout at him but know there's no point. "Yvette was here in our bed. She wants you for her husband or lover. I told you she had a scheme."

He looks down at the pistol on the floor and sees the trail of blood. "Lalin, are you hurt? Are you wounded?"

"No, but she is. The gun fired off and hit her in the arm."

"Did I shoot her?" he asks.

"It was me, but the damage can't be serious. She shifted to her bird form and flew away."

He makes a groan deep in his throat. "I feel like a fool, like a hopeless fool. What's happening to me? First, I'm cursed with this loup garou affliction. And then that woman's able to attack me and I remember nothing."

His distress makes me sad. I've never seen him cry, but the way he drops his eyes to the floor tells me he's holding back his tears. She's managed to have her way with him. It's very hard for me to face that. I must be strong.

"Let me get you a glass of cognac. You need something stout. I'll have a swallow too."

We sit together in my parlor, sipping cognac from my crystal glasses. Etienne's late for work. He says nothing for a long time. I ask if he would like a bowl of soup and perhaps a roll.

"I need to go. I have no appetite," he says at last. "Papa will be concerned. It's been a nightmare morning, but I have to prepare the documents for a shipment that goes out today." He turns to me, takes a deep breath and states. "The truth is that I remember little of what happened here. Please believe that the woman, Yvette, means nothing to me. Whatever she may do or say, in my heart I know I owe her nothing. She's a witch with some extraordinary powers."

I bring prayer hands to my lips. "I will make an offering to my saints. They have answers that will help us."

✳ ✳ ✳

We have no more visits from that evil, shifting bird-woman. Believe me I am watchful every minute. And the days pass quickly, as the date of Etienne's exorcism approaches. My prayers and offerings to St. Michael give me comfort. He's given me insights into the threats that linger near us.

Our enemies still conspire against us. I've made two attempts to spy on them at the house on Rue Royal. From the palm tree I saw Yvette in her boudoir with her arm bandaged and in a sling. Abel stayed in the house for several days. But now he goes out to the market by the river and frequents gambling houses in the night. I follow him in my feline form. Sometimes he loiters near the cathedral or the Presbytere. I believe he watches Father Jules from a distance. He's hampered by his own demons and cannot enter any holy place.

I also keep a watch on Dr. Lycus. Most days are taken with collecting herbs from vendors. He also spends time in the coffee houses with his notebook. For hours I observe him writing.

Today he brings a stack of books to consult as well. One thing makes me curious. Once he's settled at a table, he takes out an envelope that's stashed between the pages of one book. From where I hide behind a potted palm, I see that he removes a picture. I can only get a glimpse, but it looks to be an image of a young man. He sets it on the table, pulls out a paper from the envelope and begins to write.

Chapter Forty-Five

Tonight, we will meet our priest at the Presbytere. The ritual must take place there. Etienne can't enter any sacred places as long as he's hampered by the loup garou curse. Grandmam will meet us at the hour. Father has contacted Lycus. I also invited Apolline, as I feel her friendship will add support for me. All our trust centers on Father Jules. The full moon rises tomorrow night, and our service must take place before the phase begins.

Etienne and I stop a moment at the door. We hold each other, pressing so close I feel his heart beating. I whisper in his ear. "Faith, we must keep. The evil one will be defeated this night, my love. St. Michael always slays the dragon." I smile and hold my amulet up for him to see. His eyes widen. He has negative sensations when he's close to holy objects, so I tuck the medal back beneath the fabric of my blouse.

When he smiles back at me in relief, the tension lifts off my chest. One soft kiss against his cheek, I give him. We knock and Georgette lets us in and leads us down the hall to the study, which has been set up for the ceremony.

Our priest wears his surplice and the purple stole that's required for this rite. Father shows us the altar that he's prepared. Holy water in a vessel, a book of holy scriptures, and a crucifix are spread on the altar cloth. I hand him my silver rosary to place there too. He also brings out a container of salt, which may be used as well. I watch as Etienne backs away from the holy symbols.

Father explains the responses that must be given as he reads the Litany. The Litany of Saints comes first. While he's making sure that I know the responses in Latin, Etienne steps further back towards the office door. Father Jules and I both turn to him.

"It's a most difficult time for all of us, but most of all for you. I suggest we sip some spirits for a bit while we wait for the others," he says to Etienne.

Father Jules rings a small bell and Georgette reappears. "Please bring the decanter and the glasses."

The room has been arranged with chairs and kneelers for at least six people. It looks like a small chapel. I kneel to say prayers. Voices whisper down the hallway. It's Grandmam Selene, and Apolline, who's come with her. Father stands to invite them into the room. Georgette has placed a tray on one of the chairs. Our priest offers everyone a glass of anisette. Etienne takes a glass. He smiles at me but remains behind the chairs near the entrance to the room.

"I expect Lycus will be here any moment," Father says. "The liquor is here, if anyone wants another sip."

Grandmam puts her glass on a nearby wooden chair, takes out her rosary and kneels with her head bowed. Apolline kneels next to me and takes my hand.

"Our prayers will be answered, Lalin. I can feel the holy presence in this chamber. Father will remove the demon, loup garou."

The front door closes, and another louder voice echoes down the hall. The Dr. Lycus has arrived. He greets us brightly as if he's joining a celebration instead of an exorcism. Father Jules beckons him to one side of the room. There he shows him all the responses in Latin. I can't hear what else he says, but Lycus nods and Father pours him a glass. Apolline leaves my side and joins them in a whispered conversation.

While all these things are going on, Etienne takes another glass of anisette and walks across the room. He stands back from the altar and then returns to his position near the door, which is now closed. Just as he's reaching for the doorknob, Father Jules and Lycus jolt up so quickly that everyone is startled. I rush toward the door. Grandmam hops up from the kneeler.

All three men are at the door now. Etienne shakes his head and mutters something. He's speaks in a low voice, but then he shoves the other men away from him.

"I've changed my mind," he says. "I can't go through with this. Someone will be hurt. Have no doubt. It isn't safe." He pushes Father back again and darts through the door. As he passes through into the hall, Lycus grabs him from behind. They struggle, wrestling in the center of the entryway. Etienne shoves Lycus against, the wall.

"Help me. We must restrain him. Get the rope and handcuffs if you have them," Lycus calls out.

Father runs to a closet and seconds later comes back with the thickest rope I've ever seen. Lycus helps him drag Etienne down to the floor, but my love fights back with super strength. I run to him.

"Etienne, what're you doing? You know we're here to bring the cure for this evil."

"Get away, Lalin. It's too dangerous. The evil festers inside me. It can't be done. I must get free." He manages to get one arm loose and slams a fist at Father Jules' chin.

I can't believe what's happening. Apolline unwinds the rope for them. Lycus, who seems to have more strength than our priest, holds Etienne against the floor, while Father wraps the heavy rope around him. Grandmam helps Apolline unroll a long tablecloth from the closet. Father and Lycus roll my protector onto the fabric. He kicks with such force that it loosens up the rope.

I tell myself not to cry, while tears blur my vision. My body feels so hot. I think I'm melting. But wait, now a chill comes over me. The room begins to spin. "St. Michael help us," I cry out.

A flash of light burst through the darkness in the room. No one turns to look. It must be for my eyes only. The light hovers above the three men. Etienne continues to yell, but they're able to cover him in the cloth and then wrap another piece of rope around him. He's bound tightly now. He makes deep sounds inside his throat. His eyes look glassy.

They lift him off the floor, and carry him across the room, placing him face up in front of the altar. Father turns to us with a deep sigh, he says. "We are ready to begin."

CHAPTER FORTY-SIX

The shaft of light remains in the room, shimmering above the altar, as Father Jules begins the ritual. First, he takes the emblem of the cross, holds it over Etienne's bound body and makes the sign. With the vessel of holy water in hand, he sprinkles my protector's head.

Now he traces the cross unto Etienne's brow. My protector squirms and moans. His teeth clench he begins to grind them as Father reads slowly from the litany in Latin. We all follow with the prescribed responses. All the saints are named. Father reads psalms he's chosen from the scriptures.

Etienne strains against the ropes and begins to yell curses to the air. My body freezes. St. Michael, my Erzulie. I speak to them in whispers. The ropes around my love's ankles loosen, as he jerks his feet and legs against the floor.

Lycus moves in to wrap more rope around his feet, while Etienne yells again, rolling side to side. Our priest sprinkles more holy water from the vessel. Curses echo off the wall. The holy water sizzles when it hits my lover's skin. He screams, then twists his head, making growling sounds deep in his throat.

A vial of Etienne's blood has been placed on the altar. Father Jules opens it, murmurs more Latin prayers. He pours the blood into a small dish, then takes the vessel filled with holy water, tips it carefully so that six or eight drops mix with the blood. He stirs the liquid with a tiny silver spoon. The mixture bubbles up, as if it's boiling. The priest puts on a glove, then picks up the crucifix from the altar. Dipping the top end into the dish, he then lifts the cross high above his head, lowers it to a position above Etienne's chest and marks the sign again with blood and holy water splashing lightly against my protector's opened shirt and vest. The howl that rises from his throat would make the bravest cringe in fear.

"*Mon Dieu*, save this man," Grandmam cries out.

Father lays hands on Etienne again. The way he shudders lets me know how much he suffers from this evil. Our priest reads from the Gospels. More words in Latin, and some I can understand. He implores our God to rid this man of the demon. His voice gets louder, as Etienne's cries almost drown out his words.

"I cast you out, unclean spirit, along with every Satanic power. Begone and stay far away from this creature of God."

As he continues to demand that the Devil leave his body, the room fills with a strange haze. A stench pervades the air around us. Then comes a chill, the door flies open and a wintry wind rages through the house. The door bangs against the wall. Etienne's face grows contorted. His mouth looks twisted; his eyes roll back.

With a sudden jerk, his body rises off the floor. I think that the ropes will surely burst when he writhes there in the air. Father stands tall enough to trace the cross three times across our victim's brow.

"Begone, in the name of the Father, and of the Son, and of the Holy Spirit." There's silence now. Etienne grows quiet and drops back onto the floor. Then a loud growl splits the quiet. Louder than a lion's roar. The whole room vibrates. Glasses rattle on the tray. One candle topples over. Lycus grabs it quickly to blow out the flame. The door swings on its hinges before it slams shut. The room grows very dark before a final streak of greenish light shoots from my protector's chest. It flies around the room, making spirals in the air.

Father Jules shouts more words in Latin. The door blows open once again. Lycus moves across the room to hold it wide. Outside the Presbytere I hear the howling of the loup garou. Apolline runs to help Lycus hold the door. He tells her to press with all her strength against the powers that press to close the door. Then he rushes to the front of the building, struggles with the unseen demon to keep that exit wide open.

Father yells, "Depart hateful, evil one! You've been cast out!" The foul smell saturates the air while the dense green light circles Father. Our priest's surrounded, but the crucifix he still holds in his hands. He staggers for a minute, pushing with the symbol through the greenish mist that whirls around him.

Lycus thrusts the door against the wall so hard that the knob bursts through the plaster. He sees it anchored there. We all watch as he leaps into the swirling mist. For an instant I think surely, he will be destroyed, but his countenance changes so quickly it makes me dizzy. I see he's grown claws and fangs. And now, like a twisting vortex, Lycus and the green light rise to the ceiling. Just as suddenly they come crashing to the floor. Father casts the crucifix into the melee. A second later a silvery white light shoots up in front of Lycus. And then a sound as loud as thunder shakes the room. The demon's essence shoots down the hall and out the door into the night.

CHAPTER FORTY-SEVEN

Etienne's recovery has been slow. For five days he stayed all afternoon in our boudoir. Not able to return to his work at the shipping office, he sleeps all morning.

I went the first day to tell his papa that he'd taken ill with something like the croup. And it's true; he coughs and gags like children do when they have this sickness. His body's weak. He sits with me in the courtyard in the early evenings but grows tired quickly. At meals, he's eating very little and gets thinner every day. I fear he'll be handicapped with this frailty and never gain back all his strength.

We're blessed on the sixth day after the exorcism. There's a knocking sound on the louvered door. Only Grandmam Selene and Father Jules have been to visit. Apolline stopped in with some fruit for us, but she's been so busy selling herbs at the market that she has little time to spend.

At the door, I call out, "Who's there?"

"It's Dr. Lycus, Lalin. I must apologize for not getting here sooner."

I open the door and see that he has several packages in his hands. "I heard that Etienne's not recovering well. While it's normal to have these problems, I know you must feel much concern."

"He hardly talks, and, when he does, the coughing starts, and he grows so weak that he wants to return to the bed and sleep."

"Hmm, the possession that he suffered has left him with more difficulties than I suspected."

He blinks rapidly as he speaks. When he pauses, his lips are pressed together in one tight line. While I've grown to trust the man, I always find him intimidating. It's not that he frightens me so much as it is the mystery that he exudes.

"Don't worry so much, Lalin. I've brought several items that can be healing for his condition."

He opens one package and lays the contents on a table. "It's wolfsbane," he says. "And, as we both know, it's a potent poison in most situations, but for Etienne's affliction it will be a saving grace."

"How so?" I ask.

"Your protector's recovering from the wolf curse. Small portions of the herb will help him heal. You will see." He takes a small notebook from his pocket and thumbs through the pages. "Here, read this."

The pages that he points to describe the antidotes for the ingestion of the wolfsbane, but when I turn to the next page, there's a description of how and why it's an ancient cure for the loup garou.

It's worth a try.

"Can I keep the pages from the notebook?"

"Yes, and I'll check back to see how he's progressing." He unwraps several other packages of herbs and explains their purposes. "Please let me know through Jules, if you have questions, but I believe you'll find that he's much improved in a few days."

* * *

I thank my saints for their wisdom in letting me understand that the Dr. Lycus offers help to us. Sadly, with all the concerns I feel for Etienne and his recovery, I've not been like myself. Ordinarily, I'd prepare my own herbal treatments, but all the horrors we experienced with the ritual took a toll on me.

My main objective has been to keep my love well-nourished and let him rest. Also, to make sure that he remains safe from the witch, Yvette. I check all the doors and windows when I leave the house. All entrances must be locked.

It's been seven days by my count, and today is Sunday. I've kept him on small doses of the wolfsbane, following Lycus's notebook instructions. His strength returned with surprising quickness with this treatment.

Grandmam's stopped by on her way to early Mass at our cathedral. Etienne's already seated at the table, sipping from his cup. I pour her a cup of coffee with chicory and place a basket of hot rolls along with some plates.

"Ah, so wonderful to see you looking well again," Grandmam says, as she takes a seat at the table.

He grins and raises his cup to me. "I thank my Lalin, for all her gentle care. You and her mama did well to make this girl a perfect companion for a man. My love for her grows stronger by the day."

"I know it's true. And her love for you can't be doubted."

"We've just decided to get out of the house today. It's time." I spread butter on the rolls and then pass the basket.

Grandmam nods, with a wide smile. "May I suggest one thing?" She continues without waiting for an answer. "The spell is broken. That we know.

It's time for you to take Etienne with you to the Sunday Mass. With communion he will have a thorough cleansing that the holy spirit brings."

I turn to Etienne to see his reaction to her words. His look is thoughtful. He says nothing for several minutes. Then, "Hmm, your Grandmam Selene has made a good point, Lalin. Before the exorcism, I couldn't even enter the sanctuary. Now I can attend and enjoy the sacraments once again. Shall we dress and walk our way to be there for the noon Mass?"

I agree, but at the same time I wonder, if it's the wisest thing. The two of us seldom walk in the Quarter together. Creole men are not expected to be seen strolling with their quadroon mistresses.

✳ ✳ ✳

What happiness I feel to walk through the huge cathedral doors with my protector at my side. We haven't attended Mass together often, so many white Creoles stare at us when we come down the side aisle to take our seats in a pew. I look around, but see no one I know, and thankfully Etienne's parents are nowhere to be seen.

We kneel and pray together. Father Jules performs the rituals. When it's time to take communion, Etienne shakes his head. He motions for me to go ahead without him.

"I have to make a confession first," he whispers. "My conscience won't be clear until I've declared my sins."

In my heart I feel that his sins were washed away during the exorcism, but I will abide by his wish to make the formal confession.

After Mass ends, we take a promenade up Rue Royal to Esplanade. In this direction we don't pass the house of the loup garou. Although I feel confident that Etienne is free from their hateful spell, today I don't want us to even think of them. We walk towards the Rue de la Levee, turn there, and make our way to Rue St. Ann. The afternoon is warm with some puffy clouds drifting across the sun. We pass a few Creole couples. They whisper to each other as they see us on the banquette. I'm dressed in one of my best gowns and have a silk tignon wrapped around my head. The women tend to avert their eyes, but the men always stare. Mixed couples are especially disliked by Creole women. Since the Legendres are well known in the city, we're simply ignored.

When we pass several quadroons, also well-dressed with silk tignons, they smile at us, but no greetings are exchanged. All and all it's a quiet afternoon except for the sounds of clomping hooves resonating on the cobblestones. Only a few carriages roll pass. Some are pulled by mules, but many are horse-drawn. The wealthiest folks even have a coachman dressed in livery. They parade around the Place d'Armes on a Sunday afternoon. It's a day for leisure, perhaps some fine food and wine will come a little later.

We make our way down Rue St. Ann. The rectory stands just ahead. I'm surprised to see Father Jules coming through the front door and locking it behind him. I wave to him, and Etienne tips his hat. Father hurries down the steps and walks towards us. It's odd that he's frowning.

"Lycus just stopped here," he says. "He's quite distressed by news he's had from France. I'm on my way to help with arrangements he has to make…"

"What happened?" Etienne asks. He reaches for my hand, pulling me closer to his side.

"It all sounds bad. His son, Erwan, was arrested in the village where he lives. I don't have all the details, but he learned that the young man's jailed, and there's threats against him from the locals."

"Is there anything we can do to help?" I ask.

Our priest shrugs and shakes his head. "He received a message less than an hour ago, brought by a sailor from a ship docked on the river. I believe he's trying to get some documents and funds together to stabilize the situation. He needs to get them to the ship as soon as possible." Father steps backwards, as he speaks. I think he might break into a run. "I'll send a message, as soon as I have more news."

* * *

We've had no word from our priest about Lycus Volcain. Etienne resumes work at his papa's shipping business near the river, where he manages accounts, recruits, and entertains customers. At least ten days have passed since the ritual to rid him of the curse. He still has nightmares about shapeshifting to the loup garou. One mystery continues. He has some hairs growing in the palms of his hands.

This evening he comes in with startling news. While his travels for the business never take him too far or for very many days, a new account requires him to travel across the ocean to some islands and then to Paris, France. Although I smile when he tells me about this business, I feel my heart skip an anxious beat. He explains that he must be a way for many months. He's not sure how long.

Then he stops talking in the middle of a sentence, grabs me by the shoulders and pulls me against his chest. "I know what you're thinking, Lalin. You smile, but it's not your happy smile. You can't hide your feelings from me. The plan is…"

I interrupt, "I'm happy for you. You haven't been to France since you were a boy. It should be a lovely time, even with your business. Will your parents travel with you?"

"Oh, no, Papa will be busy here. He wants to take Mama to Paris, but not now." He tries to squeeze me tight again, but I resist.

One deep breath, I take. I feel like crying. He'll be gone so long. I have other fears too. Since he lost his wife, Minette, he's a free man, a young bachelor again. Certainly, many Creole girls would love to have him for their *Mari*. His family has wealth and all the social connections he needs to find the perfect bride. So now he goes to France, where there're so many fancy French girls. Will he not forget his Lalin? My saints, I pray, will help me with these worries. Several minutes pass, while I ponder all my sad thoughts. Etienne says nothing, but his face is happy. What's in his head? I don't like the smile he has now.

A dinner I've prepared for him, so it's time to set the table and pour some wine for us. But before I move away from him, he grabs me by the waist and lifts me off my feet. I gasp, wobbling in his arms. He whirls around like he's dancing, puts me down and kisses me with all the sweetness of his passion.

"I've told Papa," he says, "that I must take you with me on the voyage. You, *mon cher*, my love, I want you with me always."

His words startle me so much that I stumble back, staring at him. Did I hear this right? "But your papa won't agree to that. He'll not allow it!"

His brow tightens, and he frowns. "It's true; he first said *'No, impossible'*." But I stood firm and he relented. We may not be able to share a cabin on the ship, but I've convinced him that we can work things out."

I don't have to read his mind to figure out how they might resolve the question of Etienne traveling with his quadroon mistress. A journey with a servant would be permissible, but a man tours with a male valet, not a woman. Perhaps they plan to disguise me as a man.

I laugh at the thought. "Will you dress me as your man servant?"

Etienne chuckles. "We thought of that." He shakes his head. "No, no, only as a joke we thought of it. Papa's thinking that you might travel, as my assistant. He believes that we can pass you off as a clerk."

"Hmm, I'd never thought of that. I can perform healing magic with my herbs and spells, but a clerk or secretary is still a job for a man."

He nods agreement. "It's true, so it's not certain that we'll use that idea. Father thinks that he may draw up paperwork that would present you as a domestic worker, who's to be assigned a position for some relations that we have in France."

I am thrilled, of course, that they plan for me to travel with my protector. It also builds confidence for me. Monsieur Legendre's willingness to accept his son's deep affection for his octoroon mistress gives me much security in my life. I've heard that his papa always cared for his own mistress and found a marriage partner for her in later life. This will not happen to me. Etienne and I will never marry, but he has sworn to be with me for his whole life.

We enjoy our meal together tonight even more than usual. After dinner, we share another bottle of rich Bordeaux. Sitting on my sofa we cuddle close with kisses and caresses. We're almost dizzy with our passion and a little drunk. I like to tease him a bit, pushing him away, squirming when he tries to unlace my blouse. Finally, we roll off the cushions, tumbling on the carpeted floor. It's there that we consummate our love. Too many sighs to count. I wish that this coupling would never end. Such delight I can't describe. My body brims with pleasures my lover brings to me.

Chapter Forty-Eight

We've started with the preparations for our trip to France. Etienne orders one local dressmaker to make new gowns for me. I wonder that his papa allows him to spend so much. He's also contracted with a milliner to fashion fine hats to wear in the city.

I laugh when he tells me these things, because quadroons like me must always wear a tignon to cover our hair in New Orleans. Hats could be worn indoors in some places. We also wear them to sit on top of our cloth-wrapped heads. Smiling, he explains that once we leave on the ship, we are free from all such laws. And in France, I'll never need a tignon.

"The fact is, mon cher, we may walk together anywhere in Paris. We'll attend the opera there and dine out wherever we wish." He looks so happy, as he describes all the social differences that are in place in that big city.

"I am so pleased and lucky to have you as my protector!" I give him one big hug. "And my greatest joy is to see you free from all the loup garou troubles that we've had."

His smile fades when I say those words. He shrugs his shoulders and turns his face from me. I kiss his cheek and pull his chin towards me again. "Do you still suffer from the nightmares? Tell me. What's wrong? You can't hide feelings from me."

"The full moon comes around again in just a few short days." He pauses and blows a puff of air between his lips. "Two nights ago, I woke to hear a howling. You were sleeping soundly, so I slipped out of bed to check. When I walked through the parlor, I heard other sounds. There was scratching at the louvered doors and growls coming from outside on the banquette."

"You didn't open up the door, did you?"

"No, no, I froze there for minutes in the foyer. They knew I was there. That's the feeling that I had. I looked down at my palms and saw the hair still growing. I had a strong sense of hopelessness. Then I thought I must do something. I couldn't let them make me miserable again."

"I wish you'd told me when this happened. Always share your troubles with me."

"It's been a busy time with all the preparations. I didn't want you to worry," he says, looking down at his hairy palms. "I feel I'm still afflicted."

"I have the wolfsbane. Let me make a tincture for you now."

He nods, and I go straight to my cabinet of herbs and remedies. I use brandy for the mixture. After mixing it with the wolfsbane in a small pot, I light a candle to heat the blend. Later I'll use a strainer to make the finished product. The fusion must be exact, as wolfsbane can be poisonous. It's needed to give my Etienne another cleansing. I pray that he's nearly cured, but precautions must be taken. He attended the Mass without distress, but there could be something of the curse remaining.

He decides to take a short rest before returning to his office this afternoon. Although I accompany him to the boudoir, he quickly drifts off to sleep. As I lay there, I feel more and more of his distress. We thought his cure was complete. Now it appears that he may need more help. I practice breathing deeply; then quietly sliding off the bed, I leave the room.

In my parlor, I sit on the chaise longue to think. Although I have no desire to sleep, I close my eyes to communicate with St Michael. Prayers, I ask him to give me signs or visions.

As I view the room again, I feel a warmth. He's coming. I can feel it. My saint's white light begins to fill the room. What happens next is quite unexpected. Instead of the vision that I was waiting for, a loud knock rattles the outside door. I sit up with a jerk. The noise gets almost thunderous.

"I'm coming." As I make my way toward the door, I call out, "Who's there?"

The banging grows still louder. My hand reaches for the knob, but I stop and ask again. "Who is it?"

"Lycus, Dr. Lycus Volcain. Please let me in, Lalin. I need to speak with you. It's most important."

I fumble with the lock. When the door swings open, a bedraggled Dr. Lycus steps over the threshold into my foyer. Today it's not the urbane image that he normally presents. He wears his black cape, but it hangs off one shoulder. His frock coat looks rumpled, and I notice his leather boots are thick with dust. Most unusual I think to myself, as I close the door behind him.

"How are you? Can I get you coffee, Dr. Lycus?" He shakes his head, so I lead him through dining room into the parlor. I note St. Michael's light still flickers near the courtyard door. "Won't you sit down and let me take your cloak," I say. "What's this important news you've come to tell me?"

"I've bad reports from France, Lalin. My son, Erwan, has been accused of serious crimes. I've made arrangements to travel home, as soon as possible."

"Crimes? Tell me, what crimes? What happened?"

"As you know, the Volcains suffer from the curse of lycanthropy. Over many years, I've learned to manage my own problems with the malady. The wolfsbane allows me to lead a normal life. Unfortunately, Erwan's problem is more serious, and that's why I come to you." Walking across the room to the courtyard door, he stares out the glass window at the top. The white light remains, but dims. "The research I did while in New Orleans always led me to you. No one else has your expertise. We need your help."

"How so? You have collected all the herbal remedies that I can offer."

Turning from the door, he pulls a small journal from his waistcoat pocket. He opens it, and at first, I think he's about to read something directly from the pages. But instead, he pauses, thumbs through the journal, and begins to pace across the room. After several moments he stops short and begins an explanation. "You're a conjurer. I've seen you work at your meetings. And the most powerful one in the city. Many have tried to steal knowledge from you."

"I am gifted, that I know. And I've learned much from Grandmam Selene, who was the Queen of voudou magic long before I came into the title. But even with my talents, I wasn't able to save my Etienne without the help of Father Jules."

He taps his finger on the journal. "Erwan's case is different. It's clear you know yourself that your closeness to your protector made it difficult for you to help him. You need a distance from your followers. Etienne is much too close." He walks toward me, as he speaks. "Your knowledge as a priestess is what's needed in my son's curse. As a conjurer and a shifter too, you can summon and cast out the loup garou spell. I believe it's the only hope we have."

"Surely Father Jules can do more to help than me. He told us that you were upset by bad news of your son. With his faith and training, why not call on him?"

Lycus puts the journal in my hand. "Lalin, I've heard a rumor that you'll accompany Etienne to Paris soon. Word travels fast in the French Quarter. That news brought me here today. It's meant to be. Surely you see that this is no accident, no quirk of fate. Your own spirit world connected you to me. Am I right? You knew of me before we ever met. Tales of the lovely voudou Queen, who held meetings on the banks of Bayou St. John pursued me up and down the river when I first arrived in this country. Read these notes I wrote many months ago. The proof is here."

He's right. The connection, the link between us, has been there all along. He frightened me at first, wrapped in his black cape, so tall and imposing, he looked. That first vision of him on his black stallion on the bayou road alarmed me. I hid, trembled at the sight of him. The King of Loup Garou was what I feared. It's taken almost a year to build up a trust of him.

"There's truth in what you say, but I can't help thinking that the priest can offer more than me in such a case of demon spirits."

"The difference is that we were born into the curse. Your protector was a victim of the loup garou, Abel. The church could bring some saving grace to Etienne. For Erwan and I, it doesn't offer a solution. It's in our blood. He has more hope of healing through a voudou ritual. I believe your conjuring could save him from the threats of lynching."

Chapter Forty-Nine

Mon Dieu, I can't believe we're standing on the docks, watching while our trunks are loaded on the ship. I turn to see Grandmam Selene crossing Rue de Levee to say her last good-byes to us. A small basket she carries, the handle hooked through her forearm. She knows I'll see my mama too on this trip. Mama travels with her rich protector in the south of France, but she's set a date to meet me in the city.

I wave to Grandmam and nudge Etienne to see her too. She looks frail this morning. I worry that she'll catch a sickness while I'm away. But Apolline has promised to check on her most days. We greet each other with warm hugs. Etienne gives her a sweet kiss on the cheek. She hands me the basket filled with calla cakes and rolls.

"Eat these and think of me," she says, laughing.

"I wish you were coming with us." I give her another hug. "Mama writes that she plans to come back to New Orleans soon and bring you back to Paris with her."

"Ha! We'll see on that one." She smiles, but a few tears show in the corners of her eyes. "Don't stay away too long, mon cher."

"I will write. Watch for my letters."

A loud voice sounds from near the gangplank. We're called to board the ship. One more hug for Grandmam. Etienne takes my hand. "It's time to go, Lalin."

Our heels click against the boards, as we proceed up the gangplank to the ship's deck. I see three of my followers running up the dockside. Our last bayou meeting took place only one week ago. Many of my people came to plead with me not to leave them without help. Some cried when I told them I would be away for months. It took me much time to explain how I had trained Apolline. With her assistance, they will still have the benefits of my healing remedies. So, it is that they accept my departure. Now they wave to us and call out blessings, as the last of the passengers and supplies are loaded. The gangplank's removed, so that we can sail off towards the Gulf of Mexico and then on across the ocean.

A deckhand helps the passengers to find their cabins. Etienne and I separate, but he thinks there'll be no problem as soon as we leave the city. The laws here work against us. Still I am fortunate that I have him as my protector. Many are not so lucky as I am.

Dr. Lycus boarded this ship before us. We had a brief conversation on the dock. Once the ship sails into the open waters, we'll be free to dine together. An early dinner we'll make of it.

* * *

A long day it's been. The conversation we had with Lycus this afternoon was quite intense. He tells us that it's his belief that Etienne must take the wolfsbane potions for many months and perhaps years. The full moon has come and gone. Although my love suffered some changes in his demeanor for a few hours, he got through the night without major problems. But there are signs that he's not completely cured. It's like the demon left some type of sickness that lingers in his body.

Our enemies roamed the Quarter that night. We heard them howling. Reports that a woman had been attacked near Rue Burgundy circulated around the city. While no one's mentioned seeing the giant bird, I believe that Yvette's always nearby. In fact, I've even worried that they might try to board the ship we're now on. Both Lycus and Etienne say they were able to check the passenger and crew lists. We should be safe.

We'll have many days at sea. I've brought a satchel full of herbs to keep me busy making medicines to use in healing. Etienne brought ledgers and charts from the shipping office to work on. Dr. Lycus claims he's writing a book about what he's learned in his travels. We also plan to work together on some remedies and rituals to save his son, Erwan.

*   *   *

Evening clouds fade from magenta into dusky blue, as our sun sets in its royal hues. The horizon presents a violet-colored canvas, edged with shades of gold, glinting on the dark gulf waters. What a sunset to remember on our departure! All the rainbow tones I could imagine, deepening as they blend into the nighttime sky.

My love and I stroll the deck, arm, and arm. I wear my hair loose. No tignon needed here. A light shawl around my shoulders is lifted by the breeze. We stop near the ship's bow. The scent of saltwater floats to my nose. A flock of seagulls cries above, gliding off toward some small island in the gulf. The seas are calm. Small waves splash against the bow. I think most passengers must be relaxing in their cabins. Only a few crew members perform tasks on the deck.

"At last a sense of peacefulness," Etienne whispers in my ear.

"Yes, I feel it too. I've never been so far from home before, but I know I'm safe with you." I rub his cheek with my fingers. He leans down to kiss me lightly on the lips.

"I'm happy that you are here with me, Lalin. I couldn't bear to be away from you for so many months."

"We'll be together with work to do, my love. I only worry that we face so many trials when we reach our destination. I pray my saints will guide us through all the days ahead."

ABOUT THE AUTHOR

MARGARET O. HOWARD is the author of the novel, *Lalin Bonheur.* In her new book, *Bewitched by Talons,* she continues the magical story of the young voudou queen, Lalin. Although it's been many years since she lived in New Orleans, she loves to visit and research the city's history for her books.

Margaret has two grown sons. She adores family gatherings, sharing with friends, books, photography, traveling, and walking on the beach in cool weather. Currently, she lives across the road from the Gulf beaches of North Florida with her two rescue cats.